2013 SUPPLEMENT TO
CONSTITUTIONAL LAW
CASES—COMMENTS—QUESTIONS

Eleventh Edition

■ ■ ■

By

Jesse H. Choper
Earl Warren Professor of Public Law,
University of California, Berkeley

Richard H. Fallon, Jr.
Ralph S. Tyler, Jr. Professor of Constitutional Law,
Harvard University

Yale Kamisar
Professor Emeritus of Law, University of San Diego
Clarence Darrow Distinguished University Professor Emeritus of Law,
University of Michigan

Steven H. Shiffrin
Charles Frank Reavis, Sr., Professor of Law,
Cornell University

AMERICAN CASEBOOK SERIES®

WEST®

Mat #41465836

American Casebook Series is a trademark registered in the U.S. Patent and Trademark Office.

© West, a Thomson business, 2006–2008
© 2009, 2010, 2011, 2012 Thomson Reuters
© 2013 LEG, Inc. d/b/a West Academic Publishing

    610 Opperman Drive
    St. Paul, MN 55123
    1-800-313-9378

West, West Academic Publishing, and West Academic are trademarks of West Publishing Corporation, used under license.

Printed in the United States of America

ISBN: 978–0–314–28846–2

PREFACE

This Supplement contains all significant United States Supreme Court cases decided since publication of the principal book. The editorial style follows that of the principal book. Chapter and section titles from the principal books have been reproduced in this Supplement to facilitate identification of the material to be inserted.

JESSE H. CHOPER
RICHARD H. FALLON, JR.
YALE KAMISAR
STEVEN H. SHIFFRIN

July 2013

TABLE OF CONTENTS

TABLE OF CASES

The principal cases are in bold type.

2013 SUPPLEMENT TO
CONSTITUTIONAL LAW
CASES—COMMENTS—QUESTIONS

Eleventh Edition

CHAPTER 1

NATURE AND SCOPE OF JUDICIAL REVIEW

■ ■ ■

SECTION 2. POLITICAL QUESTIONS

P. 46, at end of note 6

(d) ZIVOTOFSKY v. CLINTON, 132 S.Ct. 1421 (2012), per ROBERTS, C.J., rejected political question objections and held that the federal courts could determine the constitutionality of a statute requiring the State Department to list "Israel" as the place of birth on the passports of Americans born in Jerusalem who requested that listing. The State Department refused to comply with the law on the ground that, by purporting to recognize Jerusalem's status as part of Israel, it unconstitutionally interfered with the president's foreign affairs powers. It further argued that a suit seeking to compel compliance with the statute presented a political question. Without reference to additional factors considered in previous political question cases, the Court found that (1) there was no "textually demonstrable constitutional commitment of the issue" of the constitutionality of a federal statute to any branch other than the judiciary, and (2) "the textual, structural, and historical evidence put forward by the parties" revealed no lack of "judicially discoverable and manageable standards."

Sotomayor, J., joined in relevant part by Breyer, J., concurred, emphasizing that in "rare case[s]" the Court should find questions nonjusticiable based principally on prudential considerations, but that this was not such a case. Alito, J., also concurred separately. Breyer, J., dissented, relying on a conjunction of "prudential considerations" that included the potential foreign policy ramifications of having U.S. passports denominate Jerusalem as part of Israel when Jerusalem's status is a subject of international contention.

CHAPTER 2

NATIONAL LEGISLATIVE POWER

■ ■ ■

SECTION 1. SOURCES AND NATURE

P. 76, before note b

(aa) In UNITED STATES v. KEBODEAUX, 133 S.Ct. 2496 (2013), respondent was convicted by court-martial of a federal sex offense. After he had completed his sentence, Congress enacted a statute (SORNA) that required federal sex offenders to register in the state where they lived. By regulation, SORNA was retroactively applied to persons like respondent who had failed to reregister when he moved within Texas. The Court, per BREYER, J., noting that an earlier federal statute—predating respondent's "offense, conviction, and release from federal [custody, that] imposed upon him registration requirements very similar to those that SORNA later mandated"—fell "within the scope of Congress' authority under the Necessary and Proper Clauses":

Even though there was "conflicting evidence on the [point], Congress could reasonably conclude that registration requirements applied to federal sex offenders after their release can help protect the public from those federal sex offenders and alleviate public safety concerns. SORNA, like the earlier statute, used" conditioned "Spending Clause grants to encourage States to adopt its uniform definitions and requirements. [And] while SORNA punishes violations of its requirements (instead of violations of state law), the Federal Government has prosecuted a sex offender for violating SORNA only when that offender also violated state-registration requirements."

ROBERTS, C.J., expressing concern about the Court's discussion of "the general public safety benefits of the registration requirement," concurred only in the judgment: In *McCulloch*, "Chief Justice Marshall was emphatic that no 'great substantive and independent power' can be 'implied as incidental to other powers, or used as a means of executing them.' It is difficult to imagine a clearer example of such a 'great substantive and independent power' than the power to 'help protect the public . . . and alleviate public safety concerns.'

"* * * What matters—all that matters—is that Congress could have rationally determined that 'mak[ing] the civil registration requirement at issue here a consequence of Kebodeaux's offense' would give force to the Uniform Code of Military Justice adopted pursuant to Congress's power to regulate the Armed Forces."

ALITO , J., concurred in the judgment "solely on the ground that the registration requirement at issue is necessary and proper to execute

Congress' power '[t]o make Rules for the Government and Regulation of the land and naval forces' [because it was] designed to prevent sex offenders from avoiding registration, as many have in the past, [since] the State has no authority to require" registration after conviction in a military tribunal.

THOMAS, J., joined by Scalia, J., dissented,[b] relying on his analysis in *Comstock*: SORNA "is not directed at carrying into execution any of the federal powers enumerated in the Constitution." Neither the Spending Clause (which does not authorize regulating "individuals who have not necessarily received federal funds of any kind"), nor the Commerce Clause (because the federal statutes regulate "activity that is neither 'interstate' nor 'commercial' "), nor the Regulation of the Land and Naval Forces power (because "Congress does not retain a general police power over every person who has ever served in the military") is "aimed at protecting society from sex offenders and violent child predators." Even *Comstock* specifically relied on the fact, not present in this case, that the statute in that case "limited to individuals already 'in the custody of the' Federal Government."

SECTION 2. THE NATIONAL COMMERCE POWER

IV. NEW LIMITATIONS AT THE END OF THE 20TH CENTURY

P. 119, add footnote at end of 1st full paragraph

See Thomas, J., joined by Scalia, J., dissenting from denial of certiorari in *Alderman v. United States*, 131 S.Ct. 700 (2011): "*Scarborough* cannot be reconciled with *Lopez* because it reduces the constitutional analysis to the mere identification of a jurisdictional hook [and] could very well remove any limit on the commerce power [and] permit Congress to regulate or ban possession of any item that has ever been offered for sale or crossed state lines."

P. 132, at the end of Sec. 2

NATIONAL FEDERATION OF INDEPENDENT BUSINESS V. SEBELIUS
___ U.S. ___, 132 S.Ct. 2566, 183 L.Ed.2d 450 (2012).

CHIEF JUSTICE ROBERTS announced the judgment of the Court and delivered the opinion of the Court with respect to Parts I, II, and III–C, an opinion with respect to Part IV, in which JUSTICE BREYER and JUSTICE KAGAN join, and an opinion with respect to Parts III–A, III–B, and III–D. * * *

I. In 2010, Congress enacted the Patient Protection and Affordable Care Act [ACA]. The Act aims to increase the number of Americans covered by health insurance and decrease the cost of health care. [It does so mainly by prohibiting insurance companies from (a) denying coverage for preexisting conditions, and (b) charging unhealthy persons higher premiums than

---
[b] Scalia, J., did not join that part of this opinion that repeated the paragraphs in *Comstock* referred to in fn. a.

healthy ones.] [This] case concerns constitutional challenges to two key provisions, commonly referred to as the individual mandate and the Medicaid expansion.[a]

The individual mandate requires most Americans to maintain "minimum essential" health insurance coverage [and] those who do not comply with the mandate must make a [payment] to the Federal Government [which] the Act describes as a "penalty," calculated as a percentage of household income, subject to a floor based on a specified dollar amount and a ceiling based on the average annual premium the individual would have to pay for qualifying private health insurance. * * *[b]

[The Eleventh Circuit held that the individual mandate exceeds Congress's power under the Commerce Clause. The Sixth and D.C. Circuits reached the opposite conclusion.]

[III. A.1.] Congress has never attempted to rely on the [commerce power] to compel individuals not engaged in commerce to purchase an unwanted product.[3] [The] power to *regulate* commerce presupposes the existence of commercial activity to be regulated. If the power to "regulate" something included the power to create it, many of the provisions in the Constitution would be superfluous. For example, [the] power to regulate the armed forces or the value of money. [As] expansive as our cases construing the scope of the commerce power have been, [they] uniformly describe the power as reaching "activity" [citing, *Lopez, Perez, Jones & Laughlin*].

Wickard has long been regarded as "perhaps the most far reaching example of Commerce Clause authority over intrastate activity," but the Government's theory in this case would go much further. Under *Wickard* it is within Congress's power to regulate the market for wheat by supporting its price. But price can be supported by increasing demand as well as by decreasing supply. The aggregated decisions of some consumers not to purchase wheat have a substantial effect on the price of wheat, just as decisions not to purchase health insurance have on the price of insurance. Congress can therefore command that those not buying wheat do so, just as it argues here that it may command that those not buying health insurance do so. The farmer in *Wickard* was at least actively engaged in the production of wheat, and the Government could regulate that activity because of its effect on commerce. The Government's theory here would effectively override that limitation, by establishing that individuals may be regulated under the Commerce Clause whenever enough of them are not doing something the Government would have them do.

---

[a] The Medicaid expansion is discussed at p. 13 of this Supplement.

[b] Part II of the opinion held that the Anti–Injunction Act—which provides that "no suit for the purpose of restraining the assessment or collection of any tax shall be maintained in any court"—did not intend the payment to be treated as a "tax" for its purposes.

[3] The examples of other congressional mandates cited by Justice Ginsburg, are not to the contrary. Each of those mandates—to report for jury duty, to register for the draft, to purchase firearms in anticipation of militia service, to exchange gold currency for paper currency, and to file a tax return—are based on constitutional provisions other than the Commerce Clause.

[To] consider a different example in the health care market, many Americans do not eat a balanced diet. That group makes up a larger percentage of the total population than those without health insurance. The failure of that group to have a healthy diet increases health care costs, to a greater extent than the failure of the uninsured to purchase insurance. [Under] the Government's theory, Congress could address the diet problem by ordering everyone to buy vegetables. * * *

To an economist, perhaps, there is no difference between activity and inactivity; both have measurable economic effects on commerce. But the distinction between doing something and doing nothing would not have been lost on the Framers, who were "practical statesmen," not metaphysical philosophers, ["]dealing with the facts of political life as they understood them, putting into form the government they were creating, and prescribing in language clear and intelligible the powers that government was to take." *South Carolina v. United States*, 199 U.S. 437, 449 (1905).

[SCALIA, KENNEDY, THOMAS and ALITO, JJ., who filed a long separate dissent, other parts of which are at p. 13 of this Supplement, provided the four additional votes needed to hold the individual mandate beyond the commerce power. They further argued that "*Raich* is no precedent for what Congress has done here. That case's prohibition of growing (cf. *Wickard*), and of possession (cf. innumerable federal statutes) did not represent the expansion of the federal power to direct into a broad new field. The mandating of economic activity does.

["Moreover, *Raich* is far different from the Individual Mandate in another respect[: the] growing and possession prohibitions were the only practicable way of enabling the prohibition of interstate traffic in marijuana to be effectively enforced. Intrastate marijuana could no more be distinguished from interstate marijuana than, for example, endangered-species trophies obtained before the species was federally protected can be distinguished from trophies obtained afterwards—which made it necessary and proper to prohibit the sale of all such trophies, see *Andrus v. Allard*, 444 U. S. 51 (1979).

["With the present statute, by contrast, there are many [ways]. For instance, those who did not purchase insurance could be subjected to a surcharge when they do enter the health insurance system. Or they could be denied a full income tax credit given to those who do purchase the insurance."]

2.   The Government next contends that Congress has the power under the Necessary and Proper Clause to enact the individual mandate. [Each] of our prior cases upholding laws under that Clause involved exercises of authority derivative of, and in service to, a granted power. For example, we have upheld provisions permitting continued confinement of those already in federal custody when they could not be safely released, [*Comstock*]. The individual mandate, by contrast, vests Congress with the extraordinary ability to create the necessary predicate to the exercise of an enumerated

power. This is in no way an authority that is "narrow in scope," *Comstock*, or "incidental" to the exercise of the commerce power, *McCulloch*. Rather, such a conception of the Necessary and Proper Clause would work a substantial expansion of federal authority. No longer would Congress be limited to regulating under the Commerce Clause those who by some preexisting activity bring themselves within the sphere of federal regulation. Instead, Congress could reach beyond the natural limit of its authority and draw within its regulatory scope those who otherwise would be outside of it. Even if the individual mandate is "necessary" to the Act's insurance reforms, such an expansion of federal power is not a "proper" means for making those reforms effective. * * *c

JUSTICE GINSBURG, with whom JUSTICE SOTOMAYOR joins, and with whom JUSTICE BREYER and JUSTICE KAGAN join as to Parts I, II, III, and IV, concurring in part, concurring in the judgment in part, and dissenting in part.

I agree with The Chief Justice that the Anti–Injunction Act does not bar the Court's consideration of this case, and that the minimum coverage provision is a proper exercise of Congress' taxing power. [Unlike] The Chief Justice, however, I would hold, alternatively, that the Commerce Clause authorizes Congress to enact the minimum coverage provision. * * *

[I.] The large number of individuals without health insurance, Congress found, heavily burdens the national health-care market. [Unlike] markets for most products, however, the inability to pay for care does not mean that an uninsured individual will receive no care. Federal and state law, as well as professional obligations and embedded social norms, require hospitals and physicians to provide care when it is most needed, regardless of the patient's ability to pay. * * *

Health-care providers do not absorb these bad debts. Instead, they raise their prices, passing along the cost of uncompensated care to those who do pay reliably: the government and private insurance companies. In response, private insurers increase their premiums. [The] net result: Those with health insurance subsidize the medical care of those without it. As economists would describe what happens, the uninsured "free ride" on those who pay for health insurance. The size of this subsidy is considerable. Congress found that the cost-shifting just described "increases family [insurance] premiums by on average over $1,000 a year." * * *

The failure of individuals to acquire insurance has other deleterious effects on the health-care market. Because those without insurance generally lack access to preventative care, they do not receive treatment for conditions—like hypertension and diabetes—that can be successfully and affordably treated if diagnosed early on. When sickness finally drives the uninsured to seek care, once treatable conditions have escalated into grave health problems, requiring more costly and extensive intervention. * * *

---

c Roberts, C.J.'s opinion of the Court in Part III–C, upholding the individual mandate under the taxing power, is at p. 11 of this Supplement.

States cannot resolve the problem of the uninsured on their own. [A] universal health-care system, if adopted by an individual State, would be "bait to the needy and dependent elsewhere, encouraging them to migrate and seek a haven of repose." [To] cover the increased costs, a State would have to raise taxes, and private health-insurance companies would have to increase premiums [which] would, in turn, encourage businesses and healthy individuals to leave the State. [Facing] that risk, individual States are unlikely to take the initiative in addressing the problem of the uninsured, even though solving that problem is in all States' best interests. Congress' intervention was needed to overcome this collective action impasse.

Aware that a national solution was required, Congress could have taken over the health-insurance market by establishing a tax-and-spend federal program like Social Security. Such a program, commonly referred to as a single-payer system (where the sole payer is the Federal Government), would have left little, if any, room for private enterprise or the States. Instead of going this route, Congress enacted the ACA, a solution that retains a robust role for private insurers and state governments. * * *

In the 1990's, several States—including New York, New Jersey, Washington, Kentucky, Maine, New Hampshire, and Vermont—enacted [ACA] laws without requiring universal acquisition of insurance coverage. The results were disastrous. "All seven states suffered from skyrocketing insurance premium costs, reductions in individuals with coverage, and reductions in insurance products and providers." * * * Massachusetts, Congress was told, cracked the adverse selection problem. By requiring most residents to obtain insurance, the Commonwealth ensured that insurers would not be left with only the sick as customers.[2]

II. The Commerce Clause, it is widely acknowledged, "was the Framers' response to the central problem that gave rise to the Constitution itself." The Framers' solution[,] as they perceived it, granted Congress the authority to enact economic legislation "in all Cases for the general Interests of the Union, and also in those Cases to which the States are separately incompetent." 2 Records of the Federal Convention of 1787. * * *[a]

Consistent with the Framers' intent, we have repeatedly emphasized that Congress' authority under the Commerce Clause is dependent upon "practical" considerations, including "actual experience." *Jones & Laughlin*; see *Wickard; Lopez* (Kennedy, J., concurring). When appraising such legislation, we ask only (1) whether Congress had a "rational basis" for concluding that the regulated activity substantially affects interstate commerce, and (2) whether there is a "reasonable connection between the regulatory means selected and the asserted ends." In answering these questions, we presume the statute under review is constitutional and may

---

[2] Despite its success, Massachusetts' medical-care providers still administer substantial amounts of uncompensated care, much of that to uninsured patients from out-of-state.

[a] In their separate dissent, Scalia, Kennedy, Thomas and Alito, JJ., responded that "Article I contains no whatever-it-takes-to-solve-a-national problem power."

strike it down only on a "plain showing" that Congress acted irrationally. *Morrison*.

[Beyond] dispute, Congress had a rational basis for concluding that the uninsured, as a class, substantially affect interstate commerce. Those without insurance consume billions of dollars of health-care products and services each year. Those goods are produced, sold, and delivered largely by national and regional companies who routinely transact business across state lines. The uninsured also cross state lines to receive care. [Their] inability to pay for a significant portion of that consumption drives up market prices, foists costs on other consumers, and reduces market efficiency and stability. Given these far-reaching effects on interstate commerce, the decision to forgo insurance is hardly inconsequential or equivalent to "doing nothing"; it is, instead, an economic decision Congress has the authority to address under the Commerce Clause.

The minimum coverage provision, furthermore, bears a "reasonable connection" to Congress' goal of protecting the health-care market [by giving] individuals a strong incentive to insure. This incentive, Congress had good reason to believe, would reduce the number of uninsured and, correspondingly, mitigate the adverse impact the uninsured have on the national health-care market.

[Even] assuming, for the moment, that Congress lacks authority under the Commerce Clause to "compel individuals not engaged in commerce to purchase an unwanted product," such a limitation would be inapplicable here. Everyone will, at some point, consume health-care products and services. [But,] The Chief Justice insists, the uninsured cannot be considered active in the market for health care, because "[t]he proximity and degree of connection between the [uninsured today] and [their] subsequent commercial activity is too lacking."

This argument has multiple flaws. First, more than 60% of those without insurance visit a hospital or doctor's office each year. Nearly 90% will within five years. * * *

Equally evident, Congress has no way of separating those uninsured individuals who will need emergency medical care today (surely their consumption of medical care is sufficiently imminent) from those who will not need medical services for years to come. [See] *Perez* ("[W]hen it is necessary in order to prevent an evil to make the law embrace more than the precise thing to be prevented it may do so.")

[The] Chief Justice defines the health-care market as including only those transactions that will occur either in the next instant or within some (unspecified) proximity to the next instant. But [it] is Congress' role, not the Court's, to delineate the boundaries of the market the Legislature seeks to regulate. * * *

Third, contrary to The Chief Justice's contention, our precedent does [indeed] acknowledge Congress' authority, under the Commerce Clause, to direct the conduct of an individual today (the farmer in *Wickard*, stopped from growing excess wheat; the plaintiff in *Raich*, ordered to cease cultivating marijuana) because of a prophesied future transaction (the eventual sale of that wheat or marijuana in the interstate market). Congress' actions are even more rational in this case, where the future activity (the consumption of medical care) is certain to occur, the sole uncertainty being the time the activity will take place. * * *

Nor is it accurate to say that the minimum coverage provision "compel[s] individuals . . . to purchase an unwanted product." [Virtually] everyone, I reiterate, consumes health care at some point in his or her life. * * *

At bottom, The Chief Justice's and the joint dissenters' "view that an individual cannot be subject to Commerce Clause regulation absent voluntary, affirmative acts that enter him or her into, or affect, the interstate market expresses a concern for individual liberty that [is] more redolent of Due Process Clause arguments." Plaintiffs have abandoned any argument pinned to substantive due process, however, and now concede that the provisions here at issue do not offend the Due Process Clause.

Underlying The Chief Justice's view [is] a fear that the commerce power would otherwise know no limits. [But] the unique attributes of the health-care market render everyone active in that market and give rise to a significant free-riding problem that does not occur in other markets. * * *

Supplementing these legal restraints is a formidable check on congressional power: the democratic process. As the controversy surrounding the passage of the Affordable Care Act attests, purchase mandates are likely to engender political resistance. [Additionally the Chief Justice] emphasizes the provision's novelty. [But as] our national economy grows and changes, we have recognized, Congress must adapt to the changing "economic and financial realities." Hindering Congress' ability to do so is shortsighted; if history is any guide, today's constriction of the Commerce Clause will not endure. * * *

[III.]   Asserting that the Necessary and Proper Clause does not authorize the minimum coverage provision, The Chief Justice focuses on the word "proper." A mandate to purchase health insurance is not "proper" [because] it is less "narrow in scope" than other laws this Court has upheld under the Necessary and Proper Clause (citing *Comstock*). [But how] is a judge to decide, when ruling on the constitutionality of a federal statute, whether Congress employed an "independent power," or merely a "derivative" one? Whether the power used is "substantive," or just "incidental"? The instruction The Chief Justice, in effect, provides lower courts: You will know it when you see it. * * *

SECTION 3. THE NATIONAL TAXING AND SPENDING POWERS

I. REGULATION THROUGH TAXING

P. 135, at the end of note 3

In NATIONAL FEDERATION OF INDEPENDENT BUSINESS v. SEBELIUS, p. 4 of this Supplement, Part III–C of ROBERTS, C.J.'s opinion for the Court held that the "exaction the Affordable Care Act imposes on those without health insurance looks like a tax in many respects. The [individual mandate payment] is paid to the Treasury by 'taxpayer[s]' when they file their tax returns. It does not apply to individuals who do not pay federal income taxes because their household income is less the threshold in the Internal Revenue Code. For taxpayers who do owe the payment, its amount is determined by such familiar factors as taxable income, number of dependents, and joint filing status. The requirement to pay is found in the Internal Revenue Code and enforced by the IRS, [which] must assess and collect it 'in the same manner as taxes.' This process yields the essential feature of any tax: it produces at least some revenue for the Government. *Kahriger.* Indeed, the payment is expected to raise about $4 billion per year by 2017.

"It is of course true that the Act describes the payment as a 'penalty,' not a 'tax.' But that label [does] not determine whether the payment may be viewed as an exercise of Congress's taxing power. * * *

"Our precedent reflects this. [See] *Nelson v. Sears, Roebuck & Co.,* 312 U. S. 359, 363 (1941) ("In passing on the constitutionality of a tax law, we are concerned only with its practical operation, not its definition or the precise form of descriptive words which may be applied to it"); *United States v. Sotelo,* 436 U. S. 268, 275 (1978) ("That the funds due are referred to as a 'penalty' does not alter their essential character as taxes"). * * *[7]

The same analysis here suggests that the [individual mandate] payment may for constitutional purposes be considered a tax, not a penalty: First, for most Americans the amount due will be far less than the price of insurance, and, by statute, it can never be more.[8] It may often be a reasonable financial decision to make the payment rather than purchase insurance, unlike the 'prohibitory' financial punishment in the *Child Labor Tax Case.* Second, the individual mandate contains no scienter requirement. Third, the payment is collected solely by the IRS through the normal means of taxation—except that the Service is not allowed to use those means most suggestive of a punitive sanction, such as criminal prosecution. * * *

---

[7] *Sotelo,* in particular, would seem to refute the joint dissent's contention that we have "never" treated an exaction as a tax if it was denominated a penalty. * * *

[8] In 2016, for example, individuals making $35,000 a year are expected to owe the IRS about $60 for any month in which they do not have health insurance. Someone with an annual income of $100,000 a year would likely owe about $200. The price of a qualifying insurance policy is projected to be around $400 per month.

"None of this is to say that the payment is not intended to affect individual conduct. Although the payment will raise considerable revenue, it is plainly designed to expand health insurance coverage. But taxes that seek to influence conduct are nothing new. [Today,] federal and state taxes can compose more than half the retail price of cigarettes, not just to raise more money, but to encourage people to quit smoking. And we have upheld such obviously regulatory measures as taxes on selling marijuana and sawed-off shotguns. See *Sanchez; Sonzinsky.* * * *

"Indeed, it is estimated that four million people each year will choose to pay the IRS rather than buy insurance. [That] Congress apparently regards such extensive failure to comply with the mandate as tolerable suggests that Congress did not think it was creating four million outlaws. It suggests instead that the [individual mandate] payment merely imposes a tax citizens may lawfully choose to pay in lieu of buying health insurance. * * *

[The Court also rejected the argument that the individual mandate violates the Direct Tax Clause, Art. 1, § 9, ch. 4.]

"There may, however, be a more fundamental objection to a tax on those who lack health insurance. [The] Court today holds that our Constitution protects us from federal regulation under the Commerce Clause so long as we abstain from the regulated activity. [But] Congress's use of the Taxing Clause to encourage buying something is, by contrast, not new. Tax incentives already promote, for example, purchasing homes and professional educations. * * *

"Second, Congress's ability to use its taxing power to influence conduct is not without limits. [See *Child Labor Tax Case.* More] recently we have declined to closely examine the regulatory motive or effect of revenue-raising measures. See *Kahriger,* (collecting cases). We have nonetheless maintained that 'there comes a time in the extension of the penalizing features of the so-called tax when it loses its character as such and becomes a mere penalty with the characteristics of regulation and punishment.' *Department of Revenue of Mont. v. Kurth Ranch,* 511 U.S., at 779 (1994).

"We have already explained that the [individual mandate] payment's practical characteristics pass muster as a tax under our narrowest interpretations of the taxing power. Because the tax at hand is within even those strict limits, we need not here decide the precise point at which an exaction becomes so punitive that the taxing power does not authorize it. * * *

"Third, although the breadth of Congress's power to tax is greater than its power to regulate commerce, the taxing power does not give Congress the same degree of control over individual behavior. [It] is limited to requiring an individual to pay money into the Federal Treasury, no more. If a tax is properly paid, the Government has no power to compel or punish individuals subject to it. We do not make light of the severe burden that taxation— especially taxation motivated by a regulatory purpose—can impose. But imposition of a tax nonetheless leaves an individual with a lawful choice to do or not do a certain act, so long as he is willing to pay a tax levied on that choice."

SCALIA, KENNEDY, THOMAS and ALITO JJ., dissented: The individual mandate "challenged under the Constitution is either a penalty or else a tax. Of course in many cases what was a regulatory mandate enforced by a penalty *could have been* imposed as a tax upon permissible action; or what was imposed as a tax upon permissible action *could have been* a regulatory mandate enforced by a penalty. But we know of no case [in] which the imposition was, for constitutional purposes, both. [The] issue is not whether Congress had the *power* to frame the minimum-coverage provision as a tax, but whether it *did* so.

"[In] this case, there is simply no way, 'without doing violence to the fair meaning of the words used' to escape what Congress enacted: a mandate that individuals maintain minimum essential coverage, enforced by a penalty. [We] have never held that any exaction imposed for violation of the law is an exercise of Congress' taxing power—even when the statute calls it a tax, much less when (as here) the statute repeatedly *calls* it a penalty. * * *

"So the question is, quite simply, whether the exaction here is imposed for violation of the law. It unquestionably is. [T]hat Congress (in its own words) 'imposed . . . a penalty' for failure to buy insurance is alone sufficient to render that failure unlawful. [W]e have never—*never*—treated as a tax an exaction which faces up to the critical difference between a tax and a penalty, and explicitly denominates the exaction a 'penalty.' Eighteen times in § 5000A itself and else-where throughout the Act, Congress called the exaction in § 5000A(b) a 'penalty.' [T]he nail in the coffin is that the mandate and penalty are located in Title I of the Act, its operative core, rather than where a tax would be found—in Title IX, containing the Act's 'Revenue Provisions.' In sum, 'the terms of [the] act rende[r] it unavoidable.' "

II. REGULATION THROUGH SPENDING

P. 141, after note 1

In NATIONAL FEDERATION OF INDEPENDENT BUSINESS v. SEBELIUS, p. 4 of this Supplement, Part IV of ROBERTS, C.J.'s opinion addressed the ACA's "Medicaid expansion": "The States also contend that the Medicaid expansion exceeds Congress's authority under the Spending Clause. They claim that Congress is coercing the States to adopt the changes it wants by threatening to withhold all of a State's Medicaid grants, unless the State accepts the new expanded funding and complies with the conditions that come with it.

"[The] current Medicaid program requires States to cover only certain discrete categories of needy individuals—pregnant women, children, needy families, the blind, the elderly, and the disabled. [On] average States cover only those unemployed parents who make less than 37 percent of the federal poverty level, and only those employed parents who make less than 63 percent of the poverty line.

"The Medicaid provisions of the Affordable Care Act, in contrast, require States to expand their Medicaid programs by 2014 to cover all individuals under the age of 65 with incomes below 133 percent of the federal poverty line. The Act [also] provides that the Federal Government will pay 100 percent of the costs of covering these newly eligible individuals through 2016. In the following years, the federal payment level gradually decreases, to a minimum of 90 percent. In light of the expansion in coverage mandated by the Act, the Federal Government estimates that its Medicaid spending will increase by approximately $100 billion per year, nearly 40 percent above current levels.

"[O]ur cases have recognized limits on Congress's power under the Spending Clause to secure state compliance with federal objectives. [Congress] may use its spending power to create incentives for States to act in accordance with federal policies. But when 'pressure turns into compulsion,' *Steward Machine*, the legislation [would] threaten the political accountability key to our federal system. '[W]here the Federal Government directs the States to regulate, it may be state officials who will bear the brunt of public disapproval, while the federal officials who devised the regulatory program may remain insulated from the electoral ramifications of their decision.' *New York v. United States.* [T]his danger is heightened when Congress acts under the Spending Clause, because Congress can use that power to implement federal policy it could not impose directly under its enumerated powers. * * *

"The States [argue] that the Medicaid expansion is far from the typical case [in] the way it has structured the funding: Instead of simply refusing to grant the new funds to States that will not accept the new conditions, Congress has also threatened to withhold those States' existing Medicaid funds. The States claim that this threat serves no purpose other than to force unwilling States to sign up for the dramatic expansion in health care coverage effected by the Act.

"[In *Dole*,] we found that the inducement was not impermissibly coercive, because Congress was offering only 'relatively mild encouragement to the States.' We observed that 'all South Dakota would lose if she adheres to her chosen course as to a suitable minimum drinking age is 5%' of her highway funds. In fact, the federal funds at stake constituted less than half of one percent of South Dakota's budget at the time. * * *

"In this case, the financial 'inducement' Congress has chosen is much more than 'relatively mild encouragement'—it is a gun to the head. [A] State that opts out of the Affordable Care Act's expansion in health care coverage thus stands to lose not merely 'a relatively small percentage' of its existing Medicaid funding, but *all* of it. Medicaid spending accounts for over 20 percent of the average State's total budget, with federal funds covering 50 to 83 percent of those costs.

"[T]he Government claims that the Medicaid expansion is properly viewed merely as a modification of the existing program because [the] original Medicaid provisions contain a clause expressly reserving '[t]he right to alter, amend, or repeal any provision' of that statute. So it does. But [a] State confronted with statutory language reserving the right to 'alter' or 'amend' [might] reasonably assume that Congress was entitled to make adjustments to the Medicaid program as it developed. [The] Medicaid expansion, however, accomplishes a shift in kind, not merely degree. [It] is no longer a program to care for the neediest among us, but rather an element of a comprehensive national plan to provide universal health insurance coverage.[14] * * *

"The Court in *Steward Machine* did not attempt to 'fix the outermost line' where persuasion gives way to coercion. [We] have no need to fix a line either.[a] It is enough for today that wherever that line may be, this statute is surely beyond it."[b]

GINSBURG, J., joined by Sotomayor, J., dissented: The Chief Justice *"for the first time ever*—finds an exercise of Congress' spending power unconstitutionally coercive.

"Medicaid, as amended by the ACA, however, is not two spending programs; it is a single [program]. Given past expansions, plus express statutory warning that Congress may change the requirements participating States must meet, there can be no tenable claim that the ACA fails for lack of [notice.] Congress is simply requiring States to do what States have long been required to do to receive Medicaid funding: comply with the conditions Congress prescribes for participation. [Even] if courts were inclined to second-guess Congress' conception of the character of its legislation, how would reviewing judges divine whether an Act of Congress, purporting to amend a law, is in reality not an amendment, but a new creation? At what point does an extension become so large that it 'transforms' the basic law? * * *

---

[14] Justice Ginsburg suggests that the States can have no objection to the Medicaid expansion, because "Congress could have repealed Medicaid [and,] [t]hereafter, could have enacted Medicaid II, a new program combining the pre–2010 coverage with the expanded coverage required by the ACA." But it would certainly not be that easy. Practical constraints would plainly inhibit, if not preclude, [putting] every feature of Medicaid on the table for political reconsideration. * * *

[a] The joint opinion of Scalia, Kennedy, Thomas, and Alito, JJ., dissenting, added that "whether federal spending legislation crosses the line from enticement to coercion is often difficult to determine, and courts should not conclude that legislation is unconstitutional on this ground unless the coercive nature of an offer is unmistakably clear. In this case, however, there can be no doubt."

[b] Roberts, C.J. held that under the ACA's severability clause, Congress intended that, if the Medicaid expansion were found the unconstitutional, it would be fully remedied by permitting the states that wished to do so to decline the federal funding for the expansion without having *all* federal funding for Medicaid withdrawn. Ginsburg, J., joined by Sotomayor, J., who dissented on the merits (see below), agreed with Roberts, C.J.'s view that "the Medicaid's severability clause determines the appropriate remedy." The joint dissent of Scalia Kennedy, Thomas and Alito, JJ., would invalidate the expansion in full, and since they would find that both the individual mandate and the expansion are invalid, "all other provisions of the Act must fail as well."

"Since 1965, Congress has amended the Medicaid program on more than 50 occasions, sometimes quite sizably. Most relevant here, between 1988 and 1990, Congress [added] millions to the Medicaid-eligible population. Between 1966 and 1990, annual federal Medicaid spending grew from $631.6 million to $42.6 billion; state spending rose to $31 billion over the same period. * * *

"Compared to past alterations, the ACA is notable for the extent to which the Federal Government will pick up the tab. Medicaid's 2010 expansion is financed largely by federal outlays. [Through] 2014, federal funds will cover 100% of the costs for newly eligible beneficiaries; that rate will gradually decrease before settling at 90% in 2020. [The] Congressional Budget Office (CBO) projects that States will spend 0.8% more than they would have, absent the [ACA.] Whatever the increase in state obligations after the ACA, it will pale in comparison to the increase in federal funding.

"Finally, any fair appraisal of Medicaid would require acknowledgment of the considerable autonomy States enjoy under the [Act.] States, as first-line administrators, will continue to guide the distribution of substantial resources among their needy populations. [U]ndoubtedly the interests of federalism are better served when States retain a meaningful role in the implementation of a program of such importance.[17]

"The Chief Justice appears to find [a] requirement that, when spending legislation is first passed, or when States first enlist in the federal program, Congress must provide clear notice of conditions it might later impose. If I understand his point correctly, it was incumbent on Congress, in 1965, to warn the States clearly of the size and shape potential changes to Medicaid might take. And absent such notice, sizable changes could not be made mandatory. Our decisions do not support such a requirement.

"[In] *Bowen v. Public Agencies Opposed to Social Security Entrapment*, 477 U.S. 41, 51–52 (1986), [Congress] changed Social Security from a program voluntary for the States [to cover their employees] to one from which they could not escape. [By] including in the Act 'a clause expressly reserving to it "[t]he right to alter, amend, or repeal any provision" of the Act,' we [unanimously] held, Congress put States on notice that the Act 'created no contractual rights.' As *Bowen* indicates, no State could reasonably have read § 1304 [of the Medicaid Act] as reserving to Congress authority to make adjustments only if modestly sized. [In] short, given § 1304, this Court's construction of § 1304's language in *Bowen*, and the enlargement of Medicaid in the years since 1965, a State would be hard put to complain that it lacked fair notice when, in 2010, Congress altered Medicaid to embrace a larger portion of the Nation's poor. * * *

"When future Spending Clause challenges arrive, as they likely will in the wake of today's decision, how will litigants and judges assess whether 'a State has a legitimate choice whether to accept the federal conditions in

---

[17] The Chief Justice and the joint dissenters perceive in cooperative federalism a "threa[t]" to "political accountability." [But] Medicaid's status as a federally funded, state-administered program is hardly hidden from view.

exchange for federal funds'? Are courts to measure the number of dollars the Federal Government might withhold for noncompliance? The portion of the State's budget at stake? And which State's—or States'—budget is determinative: the lead plaintiff, all challenging States (26 in this case, many with quite different fiscal situations), or some national median? Does it matter [that] the coercion state officials in fact fear is punishment at the ballot box for turning down a politically popular federal grant? [The] coercion inquiry, therefore, appears to involve political judgments that defy judicial calculation."

CHAPTER 4

STATE POWER TO REGULATE

■ ■ ■

SECTION 4. INTERSTATE PRIVILEGES AND IMMUNITIES CLAUSE

P. 333, at end of note 1

McBURNEY v. YOUNG, 133 S.Ct. 1709 (2013), per ALITO, J., unanimously rejected an argument that Virginia's Freedom of Information Act (FOIA) violated the Privileges and Immunities Clause by granting Virginia citizens, but not out-of-staters, access to all public records: "Petitioners allege that Virginia's citizens-only FOIA provision violates four different 'fundamental' privileges or immunities: the opportunity to pursue a common calling, the ability to own and transfer property, access to the Virginia courts, and access to public information. [Although t]he challenged provision has the incidental effect of preventing citizens of other States from making a profit by trading on information contained in state records, [the] Court has struck laws down as violating the privilege of pursuing a common calling only when those laws were enacted for the protectionist purpose of burdening out-of-state citizens. [Here,] the distinction that the statute makes between citizens and noncitizens has a distinctly nonprotectionist aim. The state FOIA essentially represents a mechanism by which those who ultimately hold sovereign power (i.e., the citizens of the Commonwealth) may obtain an accounting from the public officials to whom they delegate the exercise of that power.

"[If] a State prevented out-of-state citizens from accessing records—like title documents and mortgage records—that are necessary to the transfer of property, the State might well run afoul of the Privileges and Immunities Clause. Virginia, however, does not prevent citizens of other States from obtaining such documents. [Requiring] noncitizens to conduct a few minutes of Internet research in lieu of using a relatively cumbersome state FOIA process cannot be said to impose any significant burden on noncitizens' ability to own or transfer property in Virginia.

"[Although] the Privileges and Immunities Clause 'secures citizens of one State the right to resort to the courts of another, equally with the citizens of the latter State,' [the] Court has made clear that 'the constitutional requirement is satisfied if the non-resident is given access [upon] terms which in themselves are reasonable and adequate. [Virginia's] rules of civil procedure provide for both discovery and subpoenas duces tecum. There is no

19

reason to think that those mechanisms are insufficient to provide noncitizens with any relevant, nonprivileged documents needed in litigation.

"Finally, we [cannot] agree that the Privileges and Immunities Clause covers [a] broad right [of access to public information]. No such right was recognized at common law. [Nor] is such a sweeping right 'basic to the maintenance or well-being of the Union.'

"[Petitioners' dormant Commerce Clause challenge also fails because] Virginia's FOIA law neither 'regulates' nor 'burdens' interstate commerce; rather, it merely provides a service to local citizens that would not otherwise be available at all."

CHAPTER 6

PROTECTION OF INDIVIDUAL RIGHTS: DUE PROCESS, THE BILL OF RIGHTS, AND NONTEXTUAL CONSTITUTIONAL RIGHTS

■ ■ ■

SECTION 2. THE RIGHT OF "PRIVACY" (OR "AUTONOMY" OR "PERSONHOOD")

ROE v. WADE AND THE DEBATE IT STIRRED OVER "NONINTERPRETIVIST" OR "NONORIGINALIST" CONSTITUTIONAL DECISIONMAKING

P. 448, at end of footnote a

In the four decades since *Roe*, originalism itself has evolved. Few originalist legal scholars still contend that the interpreter's task is to uncover the subjective intentions and expectations of the framers. Instead, contemporary originalists seek the original *meaning* of the Constitution, which may be inconsistent with the intentions and expectations of the framers and ratifiers. Accordingly, Professor Balkin argues that "we do not face a choice between living constitutionalism and fidelity to the original meaning of the text. They are two sides of the same coin." Jack Balkin, *Living Originalism* 20 (2011). In Balkin's view, a proper originalist understanding of the Equal Protection Clause and the Privileges or Immunities Clause of the Fourteenth Amendment guarantees a right to abortion. See id. at 214–19. Is this blurring of the lines between originalism and nonoriginalism helpful? Professor Dorf worries that "widespread acceptance of Balkin's views would allow conservatives to say that even liberals now accept originalism but then turn around and define originalism narrowly," because nothwithstanding the scholarly shift, "judges, elected officials, and the public" continue to understand originalism as a search for "the framers' and ratifiers expected applications in considering concrete cases." Michael C. Dorf, *The Undead Constitution*, 125 Harv.L.Rev. 2011, 2014 (2012).

THE *GLUCKSBERG* CASE REVISITED

P. 558, at end of note 4:

For a recent defense of the distinction between "killing" and "letting die," see Yale Kamisar, *Are the Distinctions Drawn in the Debate about End-of-Life Decision Making "Principled"? If Not, How Much Does It Matter?*, 40 J. Law, Med. & Ethics 66 (Spring 2012).

SECTION 5. THE DEATH PENALTY AND RELATED PROBLEMS: CRUEL AND UNUSUAL PUNISHMENT

IV. CONSTITUTIONAL LIMITS ON IMPOSING PUNISHMENT

P. 611, at end of Sec.

MILLER v. ALABAMA, 132 S.Ct. 2455 (2012), arose as follows: Petitioner Evan Miller, a 14–year-old, set fire to his neighbor's trailer after an evening of drinking and drug use. The neighbor died. A jury found Miller guilty and the trial court imposed a statutorily mandated punishment of life without parole. In a companion case, petitioner Kuntrell Jackson, another 14–year-old, participated in a robbery. One of the co-conspirators shot and killed the store clerk. He was charged with capital felony murder and aggravated robbery. A jury convicted him of both. The trial judge imposed a statutorily mandated punishment of life without parole. The Court, per KAGAN, J., held that the Eighth Amendment forbids a sentencing scheme that mandates life without parole sentences for juvenile homicide offenders:

"The cases before us implicate two strands of precedent reflecting our concern with proportionate punishment. The first has adopted categorical bans on sentencing practices based on mismatches between the culpability of a class of offenders and the severity of a penalty. See *Graham v. Florida*, [which] further likened life without parole for juveniles to the death penalty itself, thereby evoking a second line of our precedents. In those cases, we have prohibited mandatory imposition of capital punishment, requiring that sentencing authorities consider the characteristics of a defendant and the details of his offense before sentencing him to death. Here, the confluence of these two lines of precedent leads to the conclusion that mandatory life-without-parole sentences for juveniles violate the Eighth Amendment. * * *

"*Graham* concluded [that] life-without-parole sentences, like capital punishment, may violate the Eighth Amendment when imposed on children. To be sure, *Graham*'s flat ban on life without parole applied only to nonhomicide crimes, and the Court took care to distinguish those offenses from murder, based on both moral culpability and consequential harm. But none of what it said about children—about their distinctive (and transitory) mental traits and environmental vulnerabilities—is crime-specific. Those features are evident in the same way, and to the same degree, when (as in both cases here) a botched robbery turns into a killing. So Graham's reasoning implicates any life-without-parole sentence imposed on a juvenile, even as its categorical bar relates only to nonhomicide offenses.

"Most fundamentally, *Graham* insists that youth matters in determining the appropriateness of a lifetime of incarceration without the possibility of parole. In the circumstances there, juvenile status precluded a life-without-parole sentence, even though an adult could receive it for a similar crime.

And in other contexts as well, the characteristics of youth, and the way they weaken rationales for punishment, can render a life-without-parole sentence disproportionate. * * *

"By removing youth from the balance—by subjecting a juvenile to the same life-without-parole sentence applicable to an adult—[the mandatory penalty schemes at issue here] prohibit a sentencing authority from assessing whether the law's harshest term of imprisonment proportionately punishes a juvenile offender. That contravenes *Graham*'s (and also *Roper*'s) foundational principle: that imposition of a State's most severe penalties on juvenile offenders cannot proceed as though they were not children. And *Graham* makes plain these mandatory schemes' defects in another way: by likening life-without-parole sentences imposed on juveniles to the death penalty itself. * * *

"Mandatory life without parole for a juvenile precludes consideration of his chronological age and its hallmark features—among them, immaturity, impetuosity, and failure to appreciate risks and consequences. It prevents taking into account the family and home environment that surrounds him— and from which he cannot usually extricate himself—no matter how brutal or dysfunctional. It neglects the circumstances of the homicide offense, including the extent of his participation in the conduct and the way familial and peer pressures may have affected him. Indeed, it ignores that he might have been charged and convicted of a lesser offense if not for incompetencies associated with youth—for example, his inability to deal with police officers or prosecutors (including on a plea agreement or his incapacity to assist his own attorneys). [And] finally, this mandatory punishment disregards the possibility of rehabilitation even when the circumstances most suggest it.

"[By] making youth (and all that accompanies it) irrelevant to imposition of that harshest prison sentence, [a sentencing scheme that mandates life imprisonment without possibility of parole for juvenile offenders] poses too great a risk of disproportionate punishment. Because that holding is sufficient to decide these cases, we do not consider Jackson's and Miller's alternative argument that the Eighth Amendment requires a categorical ban on life without parole for juveniles, or at least for those 14 and younger. But given all we have said in *Roper, Graham*, and this decision about children's diminished culpability and heightened capacity for change, we think appropriate occasions for sentencing juveniles to this harshest possible penalty will be uncommon. That is especially so because of the great difficulty we noted in *Roper* and *Graham* of distinguishing at this early age between 'the juvenile offender whose crime reflects irreparable corruption.' Although we do not foreclose a sentencer's ability to make that judgment in homicide cases, we require it to take into account how children are different, and how those differences counsel against irrevocably sentencing them to a lifetime in prison."[a]

---

[a] The concurring opinion of Breyer, J., joined by Sotomayor, J., is omitted.

ROBERTS, C.J., joined by Scalia, Thomas and Alito, JJ.,[b] dissented: "The parties agree that nearly 2,500 prisoners are presently serving life sentences without the possibility of parole for murders they committed before the age of 18. The Court accepts that over 2,000 of those prisoners received that sentence because it was mandated by a legislature. And it recognizes that the Federal Government and most States impose such mandatory sentences. Put simply, if a 17–year-old is convicted of deliberately murdering an innocent victim, it is not 'unusual' for the murderer to receive a mandatory sentence of life without parole. That reality should preclude finding that mandatory life imprisonment for juvenile killers violates the Eighth Amendment.

"[The] Court notes that *Graham* found a punishment authorized in 39 jurisdictions unconstitutional, whereas the punishment it bans today is mandated in 10 fewer. But *Graham* went to considerable lengths to show that although theoretically allowed in many States, the sentences at issue in that case were 'exceedingly rare' in practice. [Here] the number of mandatory life without parole sentences for juvenile murderers, relative to the number of juveniles arrested for murder, is over 5,000 times higher than the corresponding number in *Graham*. There is thus nothing in this case like the evidence of national consensus in *Graham*.

"[In] the end, the Court does not actually conclude that mandatory life sentences for juveniles are unusual. It instead claims that precedent 'leads to' today's decision, relying on *Graham and Roper*. [But] the Court's holding does not follow from *Roper* and *Graham*. Those cases undoubtedly stand for the preposition that teenagers are less mature, less responsible, and less fixed in their ways than adults—not that a Supreme Court case was needed to establish that. What they do not stand for, and do not even suggest, is that legislators—who also know that teenagers are different from adults—may not require life without parole for juveniles who commit the worst types of murder.

"[The] Court's analysis focuses on the mandatory nature of the sentences in this case. But then—although doing so is entirely unnecessary to the rule it announces—the Court states that even when a life without parole sentence is not mandatory, 'we think appropriate occasions for sentencing juveniles to this harshest possible penalty will be uncommon.' Today's holding may be limited to mandatory sentences, but the Court has already announced that discretionary life without parole for juveniles should be 'uncommon'—or, to use a common synonym, 'unusual.'

"Indeed, the Court's gratuitous prediction appears to be nothing other than an invitation to overturn life without parole sentences imposed by juries and trial judges. If that invitation is widely accepted and such sentences for juvenile offenders do in fact become 'uncommon,' the Court will have bootstrapped its way to declaring that the Eighth Amendment absolutely prohibits them.

---

[b] Thomas, J., joined by Scalia, J. and Alito, J., joined by Scalia, J., also wrote separate dissents which are omitted.

"This process has no discernible end point—or at least none consistent with our Nation's legal traditions. *Roper* and *Graham* attempted to limit their reasoning to the circumstances they addressed—*Roper* to the death penalty, and *Graham* to nonhomicide crimes. Having cast aside those limits, the Court cannot now offer a credible substitute and does not even try. * * *

"Perhaps science and policy suggest society should show greater mercy to young killers, giving them a greater chance to reform themselves at the risk that they will kill again. But that is not our decision to make. Neither the text of the Constitution nor our precedent prohibits legislatures from requiring that juvenile murderers be sentenced to life without parole."

CHAPTER 7

FREEDOM OF EXPRESSION AND ASSOCIATION

■ ■ ■

SECTION 1. WHAT SPEECH IS NOT PROTECTED?

II. REPUTATION AND PRIVACY

D. EMOTIONAL DISTRESS

P. 716, before note 3

The father of a deceased Marine brought an action for intentional infliction of emotional distress, intrusion upon seclusion, and civil conspiracy against a fundamentalist church and its members for demonstrating near the Marine's funeral with signs whose content is detailed in the Court's opinion below, including "Thank God for Dead Soldiers."

SNYDER v. PHELPS, 131 S.Ct. 1207 (2011), per ROBERTS, C.J., held that the speech was protected and immune from tort liability: "A jury held members of the Westboro Baptist Church liable for millions of dollars in damages for picketing near a soldier's funeral service. The picket signs reflected the church's view that the United States is overly tolerant of sin and that God kills American soldiers as punishment. The question presented is whether the First Amendment shields the church members from tort liability for their speech in this case. * * *

The church had notified the authorities in advance of its intent to picket at the time of the funeral, and the picketers complied with police instructions in staging their demonstration. The picketing took place within a 10– by 25– foot plot of public land adjacent to a public street, behind a temporary fence. That plot was approximately 1,000 feet from the church where the funeral was held. Several buildings separated the picket site from the church. The Westboro picketers displayed their signs for about 30 minutes before the funeral began and sang hymns and recited Bible verses. None of the picketers entered church property or went to the cemetery. They did not yell or use profanity, and there was no violence associated with the picketing. The funeral procession passed within 200 to 300 feet of the picket site. Although Snyder testified that he could see the tops of the picket signs as he drove to the funeral, he did not see what was written on the signs until later that night, while watching a news broadcast covering the event. A few weeks after the funeral, one of the picketers posted a message on Westboro's Web site discussing the picketing and containing religiously oriented denunciations of the Snyders, interspersed among lengthy Bible quotations. Snyder discovered the posting, referred to by the parties as the 'epic,' during an Internet search for his son's name. The epic is not properly before us and does not factor in our analysis. * * *

"A trial was held on the remaining claims. At trial, Snyder described the severity of his emotional injuries. He testified that he is unable to separate the thought of his dead son from his thoughts of Westboro's picketing, and that he often becomes tearful, angry, and physically ill when he thinks about it. Expert witnesses testified that Snyder's emotional anguish had resulted in severe depression and had exacerbated pre-existing health conditions.

"To succeed on a claim for intentional infliction of emotional distress in Maryland, a plaintiff must demonstrate that the defendant intentionally or recklessly engaged in extreme and outrageous conduct that caused the plaintiff to suffer severe emotional distress. The Free Speech Clause of the First Amendment [can] serve as a defense in state tort suits, including suits for intentional infliction of emotional distress.

"Whether the First Amendment prohibits holding Westboro liable for its speech in this case turns largely on whether that speech is of public or private concern, as determined by all the circumstances of the case. '[S]peech on matters of public concern [is] at the heart of the First Amendment's protection.' * * *

" '[N]ot all speech is of equal First Amendment importance,' however, and where matters of purely private significance are at issue, First Amendment protections are often less rigorous. That is because restricting speech on purely private matters does not implicate the same constitutional concerns as limiting speech on matters of public interest: '[T]here is no threat to the free and robust debate of public issues; there is no potential interference with a meaningful dialogue of ideas'; and the 'threat of liability' does not pose the risk of 'a reaction of self-censorship' on matters of public import.

"Speech deals with matters of public concern when it can 'be fairly considered as relating to any matter of political, social, or other concern to the community,' or when it 'is a subject of legitimate news interest; that is, a subject of general interest and of value and concern to the public,' The arguably 'inappropriate or controversial character of a statement is irrelevant to the question whether it deals with a matter of public concern.' * * *

"Deciding whether speech is of public or private concern requires us to examine the 'content, form, and context' of that speech, 'as revealed by the whole record.' [In] considering content, form, and context, no factor is dispositive, and it is necessary to evaluate all the circumstances of the speech, including what was said, where it was said, and how it was said.

"The 'content' of Westboro's signs plainly relates to broad issues of interest to society at large, rather than matters of 'purely private concern.' The placards read 'God Hates the USA/Thank God for 9/11,' 'America is Doomed,' 'Don't Pray for the USA,' 'Thank God for IEDs,' 'Fag Troops,'

'Semper Fi Fags,' 'God Hates Fags,' 'Maryland Taliban,' 'Fags Doom Nations,' 'Not Blessed Just Cursed,' 'Thank God for Dead Soldiers,' 'Pope in Hell,' 'Priests Rape Boys,' 'You're Going to Hell,' and 'God Hates You.' While these messages may fall short of refined social or political commentary, the issues they highlight—the political and moral conduct of the United States and its citizens, the fate of our Nation, homosexuality in the military, and scandals involving the Catholic clergy—are matters of public import. The signs certainly convey Westboro's position on those issues, in a manner designed [to] reach as broad a public audience as possible. And even if a few of the signs-such as 'You're Going to Hell' and 'God Hates You'—were viewed as containing messages related to Matthew Snyder or the Snyders specifically, that would not change the fact that the overall thrust and dominant theme of Westboro's demonstration spoke to broader public issues.

"Apart from the content of Westboro's signs, Snyder contends that the 'context' of the speech—its connection with his son's funeral—makes the speech a matter of private rather than public concern. The fact that Westboro spoke in connection with a funeral, however, cannot by itself transform the nature of Westboro's speech. Westboro's signs, displayed on public land next to a public street, reflect the fact that the church finds much to condemn in modem society. Its speech is 'fairly characterized as constituting speech on a matter of public concern,' and the funeral setting does not alter that conclusion. * * *

"Snyder goes on to argue that Westboro's speech should be afforded less than full First Amendment protection 'not only because of the words' but also because the church members exploited the funeral 'as a platform to bring their message to a broader audience.' * * * Westboro's choice to convey its views in conjunction with Matthew Snyder's funeral made the expression of those views particularly hurtful to many, especially to Matthew's father. The record makes clear that the applicable legal term—'emotional distress'—fails to capture fully the anguish Westboro's choice added to Mr. Snyder's already incalculable grief. But Westboro conducted its picketing peacefully on matters of public concern at a public place adjacent to a public street. * * *

"Westboro's choice of where and when to conduct its picketing is not beyond the Government's regulatory reach—it is 'subject to reasonable time, place, or manner restrictions' that are consistent with the standards announced in this Court's precedents. Maryland now has a law imposing restrictions on funeral picketing. To the extent these laws are content neutral, they raise very different questions from the tort verdict at issue in this case. Maryland's law, however, was not in effect at the time of the events at issue here, so we have no occasion to consider how it might apply to facts such as those before us, or whether it or other similar regulations are constitutional.

"The record confirms that any distress occasioned by Westboro's picketing turned on the content and viewpoint of the message conveyed, rather than any interference with the funeral itself. A group of parishioners standing at the very spot where Westboro stood, holding signs that said 'God

Bless America' and 'God Loves You,' would not have been subjected to liability. It was what Westboro said that exposed it to tort damages. * * *

"Given that Westboro's speech was at a public place on a matter of public concern, that speech is entitled to 'special protection' under the First Amendment. Such speech cannot be restricted simply because it is upsetting or arouses contempt. * * *

"The jury here was instructed that it could hold Westboro liable for intentional infliction of emotional distress based on a finding that Westboro's picketing was 'outrageous.' 'Outrageousness,' however, is a highly malleable standard with an inherent subjectiveness about it which would allow a jury to impose liability on the basis of the jurors 'tastes or views, or perhaps on the basis of their dislike of a particular expression.' [What] Westboro said, in the whole context of how and where it chose to say it, is entitled to 'special protection' under the First Amendment, and that protection cannot be overcome by a jury finding that the picketing was outrageous.

"For all these reasons, the jury verdict imposing tort liability on Westboro for intentional infliction of emotional distress must be set aside.

"Our holding today is narrow. We are required in First Amendment cases to carefully review the record, and the reach of our opinion here is limited by the particular facts before us. As we have noted, 'the sensitivity and significance of the interests presented in clashes between First Amendment and [state law] rights counsel relying on limited principles that sweep no more broadly than the appropriate context of the instant case.' "[a]

BREYER, J., concurred: "I agree with the Court and join its opinion. That opinion restricts its analysis here to the matter raised in the petition for certiorari, namely, Westboro's picketing activity. The opinion does not examine in depth the effect of television broadcasting. Nor does it say anything about Internet postings. The Court holds that the First Amendment protects the picketing that occurred here, primarily because the picketing addressed matters of 'public concern.' * * *

"Westboro's means of communicating its views consisted of picketing in a place where picketing was lawful and in compliance with all police directions. The picketing could not be seen or heard from the funeral ceremony itself. And Snyder testified that he saw no more than the tops of the picketers' signs as he drove to the funeral. To uphold the application of state law in these circumstances would punish Westboro for seeking to communicate its views on matters of public concern without proportionately advancing the State's interest in protecting its citizens against severe emotional harm. Consequently, the First Amendment protects Westboro. As I read the Court's opinion, it holds no more."

ALITO, J., dissented: "Our profound national commitment to free and open debate is not a license for the vicious verbal assault that occurred in this case. Petitioner Albert Snyder is not a public figure. He is simply a parent

---

[a] The Court disposed of the other tort claims on similar grounds.

whose son, Marine Lance Corporal Matthew Snyder, was killed in Iraq. Mr. Snyder wanted what is surely the right of any parent who experiences such an incalculable loss: to bury his son in peace. But respondents, members of the Westboro Baptist Church, deprived him of that elementary right. They first issued a press release and thus turned Matthew's funeral into a tumultuous media event. They then appeared at the church, approached as closely as they could without trespassing, and launched a malevolent verbal attack on Matthew and his family at a time of acute emotional vulnerability. As a result, Albert Snyder suffered severe and lasting emotional injury. The Court now holds that the First Amendment protected respondents' right to brutalize Mr. Snyder. I cannot agree.

"Respondents and other members of their church have strong opinions on certain moral, religious, and political issues, and the First Amendment ensures that they have almost limitless opportunities to express their views. They may write and distribute books, articles, and other texts; they may create and disseminate video and audio recordings; they may circulate petitions; they may speak to individuals and groups in public forums and in any private venue that wishes to accommodate them; they may picket peacefully in countless locations; they may appear on television and speak on the radio; they may post messages on the Internet and send out e-mails. And they may express their views in terms that are 'uninhibited,' 'vehement,' and 'caustic.'

"It does not follow, however, that they may intentionally inflict severe emotional injury on private persons at a time of intense emotional sensitivity by launching vicious verbal attacks that make no contribution to public debate. To protect against such injury, 'most if not all jurisdictions' permit recovery in tort for the intentional infliction of emotional distress (or IIED). * * *

"Although the elements of the IIED tort are difficult to meet, respondents long ago abandoned any effort to show that those tough standards were not satisfied here. On appeal, they chose not to contest the sufficiency of the evidence. They did not dispute that Mr. Snyder suffered 'wounds that are truly severe and incapable of healing themselves.' Nor did they dispute that their speech was 'so outrageous in character, and so extreme in degree, as to go beyond all possible bounds of decency, and to be regarded as atrocious, and utterly intolerable in a civilized community.' Instead, they maintained that the First Amendment gave them a license to engage in such conduct. * * *

"On the morning of Matthew Snyder's funeral, respondents could have chosen to stage their protest at countless locations. They could have picketed the United States Capitol, the White House, the Supreme Court, the Pentagon, or any of the more than 5,600 military recruiting stations in this country. They could have returned to the Maryland State House or the United States Naval Academy, where they had been the day before. They could have selected any public road where pedestrians are allowed. (There are more than 4,000,000 miles of public roads in the United States.) They could have staged their protest in a public park. (There are more than 20,000 public parks in this country) They could have chosen any Catholic church where no funeral was taking place. (There are nearly 19,000 Catholic churches in the United States.) But of course, a small group picketing at any of these locations would have probably gone unnoticed.

"The Westboro Baptist Church, however, has devised a strategy that remedies this problem. As the Court notes, church members have protested at nearly 600 military funerals. They have also picketed the funerals of police officers, firefighters, and the victims of natural disasters, accidents, and shocking crimes. And in advance of these protests, they issue press releases to ensure that their protests will attract public attention.

"This strategy works because it is expected that respondents' verbal assaults will wound the family and friends of the deceased and because the media is irresistibly drawn to the sight of persons who are visibly in grief. The more outrageous the funeral protest, the more publicity the Westboro Baptist Church is able to obtain. * * *

"[T]he Court finds that 'the overall thrust and dominant theme of [their] demonstration spoke to' broad public issues. [T]his portrayal is quite inaccurate; respondents' attack on Matthew was of central importance. But in any event, I fail to see why actionable speech should be immunized simply because it is interspersed with speech that is protected. The First Amendment allows recovery for defamatory statements that are interspersed with nondefamatory statements on matters of public concern, and there is no good reason why respondents' attack on Matthew Snyder and his family should be treated differently. * * *

"[T]he Court finds it significant that respondents' protest occurred on a public street, but this fact alone should not be enough to preclude IIED liability. To be sure, statements made on a public street may be less likely to satisfy the elements of the IIED tort than statements made on private property, but there is no reason why a public street in close proximity to the scene of a funeral should be regarded as a free-fire zone in which otherwise actionable verbal attacks are shielded from liability. If the First Amendment permits the States to protect their residents from the harm inflicted by such attacks—and the Court does not hold otherwise—then the location of the tort should not be dispositive. A physical assault may occur without trespassing; it is no defense that the perpetrator had 'the right to be where [he was].' And the same should be true with respect to unprotected speech. [D]efamatory statements are [not] immunized when they occur in a public place, and there is no good reason to treat a verbal assault based on the conduct or character of a private figure like Matthew Snyder any differently.

"One final comment about the opinion of the Court is in order. The Court suggests that the wounds inflicted by vicious verbal assaults at funerals will be prevented or at least mitigated in the future by new laws that restrict picketing within a specified distance of a funeral. It is apparent, however, that the enactment of these laws is no substitute for the protection provided by the established IIED tort; according to the Court, the verbal attacks that severely wounded petitioner in this case complied with the new Maryland law regulating funeral picketing. And there is absolutely nothing to suggest that Congress and the state legislatures, in enacting these laws, intended them to displace the protection provided by the well-established IIED tort.

"The real significance of these new laws is not that they obviate the need for IIED protection. Rather, their enactment dramatically illustrates the fundamental point that funerals are unique events at which special protection against emotional assaults is in [order.] Allowing family members to have a few hours of peace without harassment does not undermine public debate. I would therefore hold that, in this setting, the First Amendment permits a private figure to recover for the intentional infliction of emotional distress caused by speech on a matter of private concern."

VI. SHOULD NEW CATEGORIES BE CREATED?

E. VIOLENT VIDEO GAMES

P. 813, before Section 2

California prohibits the sale or rental of "violent video games" to minors. The prohibition covers games "in which the range of options available to a player includes killing, maiming, dismembering, or sexually assaulting an image of a human being, if those acts are depicted" in a manner that "[a] reasonable person, considering the game as a whole, would find appeals to a deviant or morbid interest of minors," that is "patently offensive to prevailing standards in the community as to what is suitable for minors," and that "causes the game, as a whole, to lack serious literary, artistic, political, or scientific value for minors."

BROWN v. ENTERTAINMENT MERCHANTS ASS'N, 131 S.Ct. 2729 (2011), per SCALIA, J., held that the law did not meet First Amendment standards for establishing a new category of unprotected speech: "Last Term, in *Stevens,* we held that new categories of unprotected speech may not be added to the list [of unprotected categories] by a legislature that concludes certain speech is too harmful to be tolerated. [The] Government argued in *Stevens* that it could create new categories of unprotected speech by applying a 'simple balancing test' that weighs the value of a particular category of speech against its social costs and then punishes that category of speech if it fails the test. We emphatically rejected that 'startling and dangerous' proposition. [W]ithout persuasive evidence that a novel restriction on content is part of a long (if heretofore unrecognized) tradition of proscription, a legislature may not revise the 'judgment [of] the American people,' embodied in the First Amendment, 'that the benefits of its restrictions on the Government outweigh the costs.'

"That holding controls this case. As in *Stevens*, California has tried to make violent speech regulation look like obscenity regulation by appending a saving clause required for the latter. That does not suffice. Our cases have been clear that the obscenity exception to the First Amendment does not cover whatever a legislature finds shocking, but only depictions of 'sexual conduct.' Because speech about violence is not obscene, it is of no consequence that California's statute mimics the New York statute regulating obscenity-for-minors that we upheld in *Ginsberg v. New York*, [fn. e in *Miller v. California*, Sec. 1, IV, B]. That case approved a prohibition on the sale to minors of sexual material that would be obscene from the perspective of a child. We held that the legislature could 'adjus[t] the definition of obscenity "to social realities by permitting the appeal of this type of material to be assessed in terms of the sexual interests" [of] minors.' And because 'obscenity is not protected expression,' the New York statute could be sustained so long as the legislature's judgment that the proscribed materials were harmful to children 'was not irrational.'

"The California Act is something else entirely. It does not adjust the boundaries of an existing category of unprotected speech to ensure that a definition designed for adults is not uncritically applied to children. [Instead,] it wishes to create a wholly new category of content-based regulation that is permissible only for speech directed at children.

"That is unprecedented and mistaken. '[M]inors are entitled to a significant measure of First Amendment protection, and only in relatively narrow and well-defined circumstances may government bar public dissemination of protected materials to them.' No doubt a State possesses legitimate power to protect children from harm, *Ginsberg*, but that does not include a free-floating power to restrict the ideas to which children may be exposed. 'Speech that is neither obscene as to youths nor subject to some other legitimate proscription cannot be suppressed solely to protect the young from ideas or images that a legislative body thinks unsuitable for them.' *Erznoznik*.[3]

"California's argument would fare better if there were a longstanding tradition in this country of specially restricting children's access to depictions of violence, but there is [none.] California claims that video games present special problems because they are 'interactive,' in that the player participates in the violent action on screen and determines its outcome. The latter feature is nothing new: Since at least the publication of The Adventures of You: Sugarcane Island in 1969, young readers of choose-your-own-adventure stories have been able to make decisions that

---

[3] Justice Thomas ignores the holding of *Erznoznik*, and denies that persons under 18 have any constitutional right to speak or be spoken to without their parents' consent. He cites no case, state or federal, supporting this view, and to our knowledge there is none. [Scalia, J., argued that Thomas, J.'s interpretation would lead to the view that government could prevent children from attending political rallies or church without parental permission.]

determine the plot by following instructions about which page to turn to. As for the argument that video games enable participation in the violent action, that seems to us more a matter of degree than of kind.

"Justice Alito has done considerable independent research to identify video games in which 'the violence is astounding,' 'Victims are dismembered, decapitated, disemboweled, set on fire, and chopped into little pieces. . . . Blood gushes, splatters, and pools.' Justice Alito recounts all these disgusting video games in order to disgust us—but disgust is not a valid basis for restricting expression. And the same is true of Justice Alito's description of those video games he has discovered that have a racial or ethnic motive for their violence ' "ethnic cleansing" [of] African Americans, Latinos, or Jews.' To what end does he relate this? Does it somehow increase the 'aggressiveness' that California wishes to suppress? Who knows? But it does arouse the reader's ire, and the reader's desire to put an end to this horrible message. Thus, ironically, Justice Alito's argument highlights the precise danger posed by the California Act: that the *ideas* expressed by speech—whether it be violence, or gore, or racism—and not its objective effects, may be the real reason for governmental proscription.

"Because the Act imposes a restriction on the content of protected speech, it is invalid unless California can demonstrate that it passes strict scrutiny—that is, unless it is justified by a compelling government interest and is narrowly drawn to serve that interest." Scalia, J., argued that California did not meet that standard. He maintained that California could not show a causal link between violent video games and significant aggression, that courts considering the psychological evidence have found it wanting, that whatever harmful effects that do exist are indistinguishable from other unregulated media such as Saturday morning cartoon, that permitting parents to purchase violent video games for children is inconsistent with a purported concern about harmful effects, that a rating system already prevents children from purchasing many video games beyond their maturity level, and that the law is overinclusive because not all parents care about the video games their children purchase.

"California's legislation straddles the fence between (1) addressing a serious social problem and (2) helping concerned parents control their children. Both ends are legitimate, but when they affect First Amendment rights they must be pursued by means that are neither seriously underinclusive nor seriously overinclusive. As a means of protecting children from portrayals of violence, the legislation is seriously underinclusive, not only because it excludes portrayals other than video games, but also because it permits a parental or avuncular veto. And as a means of assisting concerned parents it is seriously overinclusive because it abridges the First Amendment rights of young people whose parents (and aunts and uncles) think violent video games are a harmless pastime. And the overbreadth in achieving one goal is not cured by the underbreadth in achieving the other. Legislation such as this, which is neither fish nor fowl, cannot survive strict scrutiny."

ALITO, J., joined by Roberts, C.J., concurring, argued that California's statute was unconstitutionally vague because the standards for what is inappropriate for children had been more clearly developed in the arena of sex than they have in the area of violence. He suggested that the statute would be on a stronger footing if it "targeted a narrower class of graphic depictions." At the same time, he argued that the majority was too casually dismissive of the "effect of exceptionally violent video games on impressionable minors, who often spend countless hours immersed in the alternative worlds that these games create. [When] all of the characteristics of video games are taken into account, there is certainly a reasonable basis for thinking that the experience of playing a video game may be quite different from the experience of reading a book, listening to a radio broadcast, or viewing a movie. And if this is so, then for at least some minors, the effects of playing violent video games may also be quite different. The Court acts prematurely in dismissing this possibility out of [hand.] I would hold only that the particular law at issue here fails to provide the clear notice that the Constitution requires. I would not squelch legislative efforts to deal with what is perceived by some to be a significant and developing social problem. If differently framed statutes are enacted by the States or by the Federal Government, we can consider the constitutionality of those laws when cases challenging them are presented to us."

THOMAS, J., dissenting, argued that the "Court's decision today does not comport with the original public understanding of the First Amendment. As originally understood, the First Amendment's protection against laws 'abridging the freedom of speech' did not extend to all speech. 'There are certain well-defined and narrowly limited classes of speech, the prevention and punishment of which have never been thought to raise any Constitutional problem.' Laws regulating such speech do not 'abridg[e] the freedom of speech' because such speech is understood to fall outside 'the freedom of speech.' * * *

"In my view, the 'practices and beliefs held by the Founders' reveal another category of excluded speech: speech to minor children bypassing their parents. The historical evidence shows that the founding generation believed parents had absolute authority over their minor children and expected parents to use that authority to direct the proper development of their children. It would be absurd to suggest that such a society understood 'the freedom of speech' to include a right to speak to minors (or a corresponding right of minors to access speech) without going through the minors' parents. The founding generation would not have considered it an abridgment of 'the freedom of speech' to support parental authority by restricting speech that bypasses minors' parents."

BREYER, J., dissented: "I would apply both this Court's 'vagueness' precedents and a strict form of First Amendment scrutiny. In doing so, the special First Amendment category I find relevant is not (as the Court claims) the category of 'depictions of violence,' but rather the category of 'protection of children.' This Court has held that the 'power of the state to control the conduct of children reaches beyond the scope of its authority over adults.' *Prince v. Massachusetts*, [Ch. 8, Sec. 2, I]. And the 'regulatio[n] of communication addressed to [children] need not conform to the requirements of the [F]irst [A]mendment in the same way as those applicable to adults.'

"The majority's claim that the California statute, if upheld, would create a 'new categor[y] of unprotected speech,' is overstated. No one here argues that depictions of violence, even extreme violence, *automatically* fall outside the First Amendment's protective scope as, for example, do obscenity and depictions of child pornography. We properly speak of *categories* of expression that lack protection when, like 'child pornography,' the category is broad, when it applies automatically, and when the State can prohibit everyone, including adults, from obtaining access to the material within it. But where, as here, careful analysis must precede a narrower judicial conclusion (say, denying protection to a shout of "fire" in a crowded theater, or to an effort to teach a terrorist group how to peacefully petition the United Nations), we do not normally describe the result as creating a 'new category of unprotected speech.' See *Schenck*; *Holder*.

"Thus, in *Stevens*, after rejecting the claim that *all* depictions of animal cruelty (a category) fall outside the First Amendment's protective scope, we went on to decide whether the particular statute at issue violates the First Amendment under traditional standards; and we held that, because the statute was overly broad, it was invalid. Similarly, here the issue is whether, applying traditional First Amendment standards, this statute does, or does not, pass muster.

"In my view, California's statute provides 'fair notice of what is prohibited,' and consequently it is not impermissibly vague. [Both] the *Miller* standard and the law upheld in *Ginsberg* lack perfect clarity. But that fact reflects the difficulty of the Court's long search for words capable of protecting expression without depriving the State of a legitimate constitutional power to regulate. Ultimately, [this] Court accepted the 'community standards' tests used in *Miller* and *Ginsberg*. They reflect the fact that sometimes, even when a precise standard proves elusive, it is easy enough to identify instances that fall within a legitimate regulation. And they seek to draw a line, which, while favoring free expression, will nonetheless permit a legislature to find the words necessary to accomplish a legitimate constitutional objective.

"What, then, is the difference between *Ginsberg* and *Miller* on the one hand and the California law on the other? It will often be easy to pick out cases at which California's statute directly aims, involving, say, a character who shoots out a police officer's knee, douses him with gasoline, lights him on fire, urinates on his burning body, and finally kills him with a gunshot to the head. As in *Miller* and *Ginsberg*, the California law clearly *protects* even the most violent games that possess serious literary, artistic, political, or scientific value. And it is easier here than in *Miller* or *Ginsberg* to separate the sheep from the goats at the statute's border. That is because here the industry itself has promulgated standards and created a review process, in which adults who 'typically have experience with children' assess what games are inappropriate for minors.

"There is, of course, one obvious difference: The *Ginsberg* statute concerned depictions of 'nudity,' while California's statute concerns extremely violent video games. But for purposes of vagueness, why should that matter? Justice Alito argues that the *Miller* standard sufficed because there are 'certain generally accepted norms concerning expression related to sex,' whereas there are no similarly 'accepted standards regarding the suitability of violent entertainment.' But there is no evidence that is so. The Court relied on 'community standards' in *Miller* precisely because of the difficulty of articulating 'accepted norms' about depictions of sex. I can find no difference—historical or otherwise— that is *relevant* to the vagueness question. * * *

"Like the majority, I believe that the California law must be 'narrowly tailored' to further a 'compelling interest,' without there being a 'less restrictive' alternative that would be 'at least as effective.' I would not apply this strict standard 'mechanically.' Rather, in applying it, I would evaluate the degree to which the statute injures speech-related interests, the nature of the potentially-justifying 'compelling interests,' the degree to which the statute furthers that interest, the nature and effectiveness of possible alternatives, and, in light of this evaluation, whether, overall, 'the statute works speech-related harm [out] of proportion to the benefits that the statute seeks to provide.'

"First Amendment standards applied in this way are difficult but not impossible to satisfy. Applying 'strict scrutiny' the Court has upheld restrictions on speech that, for example, ban the teaching of peaceful dispute resolution to a group on the State Department's list of terrorist organizations, *Holder*, and limit speech near polling places, *Burson* (plurality opinion). * * *

"Moreover, although the Court did not specify the 'level of scrutiny' it applied in *Ginsberg*, we have subsequently described that case as finding a 'compelling interest' in protecting children from harm sufficient to justify limitations on speech. Since the Court in *Ginsberg* specified that the statute's prohibition applied to material that was *not* obscene, I cannot dismiss *Ginsberg* on the ground that it concerned obscenity. Nor need I depend upon the fact that the Court in *Ginsberg* insisted only that the legislature have a 'rational' basis for finding the depictions there at issue harmful to children. For in this case, California has substantiated its claim of harm with considerably stronger evidence. * * *

"There are many scientific studies that support California's views. Social scientists, for example, have found *causal* evidence that playing these games results in harm. Longitudinal studies, which measure changes over time, have found that increased exposure to violent video games causes an increase in aggression over the same period. Experimental studies in laboratories have found that subjects randomly assigned to play a violent video game subsequently displayed more characteristics of aggression than those who played nonviolent games. Surveys of 8th and 9th grade students have found a correlation between playing violent video games and aggression. Cutting-edge neuroscience has shown that 'virtual violence in video game playing results in those neural patterns that are considered characteristic for aggressive cognition and behavior.' And 'meta-analyses,' i.e., studies of all the studies, have concluded that exposure to violent video games 'was positively associated with aggressive behavior, aggressive cognition, and aggressive affect,' and that 'playing violent video games is a *causal* risk factor for long-term harmful outcomes.'

"Some of these studies take care to explain in a commonsense way why video games are potentially more harmful than, say, films or books or television. In essence, they say that the closer a child's behavior comes, not to watching, but to *acting* out horrific violence, the greater the potential psychological harm. Experts debate the conclusions of all these studies. Like many, perhaps most, studies of human behavior, each study has its critics, and some of those critics have produced studies of their own in which they reach different conclusions. (I list both sets of research in the appendixes.) I, like most judges, lack the social science expertise to say definitively who is right. But associations of public health professionals who do possess that expertise have reviewed many of these studies and found a significant risk that violent video games, when compared with more passive media, are particularly likely to cause children harm. * * *

"Unlike the majority, I would find sufficient grounds in these studies and expert opinions for this Court to defer to an elected legislature's conclusion that the video games in question are particularly likely to harm children. * * * I add that the majority's different conclusion creates a serious anomaly in First Amendment law. *Ginsberg* makes clear that a State can prohibit the sale to minors of depictions of nudity; today the

Court makes clear that a State cannot prohibit the sale to minors of the most violent interactive video games. But what sense does it make to forbid selling to a 13–year-old boy a magazine with an image of a nude woman, while protecting a sale to that 13–year-old of an interactive video game in which he actively, but virtually, binds and gags the woman, then tortures and kills her? What kind of First Amendment would permit the government to protect children by restricting sales of that extremely violent video game only when the woman—bound, gagged, tortured, and killed—is also topless?

"This anomaly is not compelled by the First Amendment. It disappears once one recognizes that extreme violence, where interactive, and without literary, artistic, or similar justification, can prove at least as, if not more, harmful to children as photographs of nudity. And the record here is more than adequate to support such a view. That is why I believe that *Ginsberg* controls the outcome here a fortiori. And it is why I believe California's law is constitutional on its face."

F. STOLEN VALOR

At his first public meeting of the Three Valley Water District Board, Board Member Xavier Alvarez introduced himself: "I'm a retired marine of 25 years. I retired in the year 2001. Back in 1987, I was awarded the Congressional Medal of Honor. I got wounded many times by the same guy." These statements were false, and Alvarez was indicted under the Stolen Valor Act, 18 U.S.C. § 704 which provides that "Whoever falsely represents himself or herself, verbally or in writing, to have been awarded any decoration or medal authorized by Congress for the Armed Forces of the United States . . . shall be fined under this title, imprisoned not more than six months, or both." The Act further provides that if the false representation relates to an award of the Congressional Medal of Honor, the possible imprisonment could rise to a year.

UNITED STATES v. ALVAREZ, 132 S.Ct. 2537 (2012), held that the Stolen Valor Act violated the First Amendment. KENNEDY, J., joined by Roberts, C.J., and Ginsburg and Sotomayor, JJ., found the Act defective using the interpretive approach employed in *United States v. Stevens* and *Brown v. Entertainment Merchants Ass'n*: "In light of the substantial and expansive threats to free expression posed by content-based restrictions, this Court has rejected as 'startling and dangerous' a 'free-floating test for First Amendment coverage [based on] an ad hoc balancing of relative social costs and benefits.' *Stevens*. Instead, content-based restrictions on speech have been permitted, as a general matter, only when confined to the few 'historic and traditional categories [of expression] long familiar to the bar.' * * *

"Absent from those few categories [is] any general exception to the First Amendment for false statements. This comports with the common understanding that some false statements are inevitable if there is to be an open and vigorous expression of views in public and private conversation, expression the First Amendment guarantee. See *Sullivan* ('Th[e] erroneous statement is inevitable in free debate')."

Kennedy, J., argued that prior statements by the Court to the effect that false statements of fact have no constitutional value (see, e.g., *Gertz*), did not mean that false statements of fact were an unprotected category of speech. He maintained that the cases containing such language "all derive from cases discussing defamation, fraud, or some other legally cognizable harm associated with a false statement, such as an invasion of privacy or the costs of vexatious litigation. In those decisions the falsity of the speech at issue was not irrelevant to our analysis, but neither was it determinative. The Court has never endorsed the categorical rule the Government advances: that false statements receive no First Amendment protection. Our prior decisions have not confronted a measure, like the Stolen Valor Act, that targets falsity and nothing more. * * *

"The Government gives three examples of regulations on false speech that courts generally have found permissible: first, the criminal prohibition of a false statement made to a Government official, 18 U.S.C. § 1001; second, laws punishing perjury; and third, prohibitions on the false representation that one is speaking as a Government official or on behalf of the Government, see, e.g., § 912; § 709. These restrictions, however, do not establish a principle that all proscriptions of false statements are exempt from exacting First Amendment scrutiny. [§]1001's prohibition on false statements made to Government officials, in communications concerning official matters, does not lead to the broader proposition that false statements are unprotected when made to any person, at any time, in any context. The same point can be made about what the Court has confirmed is the 'unquestioned constitutionality of perjury statutes,' both the federal statute, § 1623, and its state-law equivalents. It is not simply because perjured statements are false that they lack First Amendment protection. Perjured testimony 'is at war with justice' because it can cause a court to render a 'judgment not resting on truth.' Perjury undermines the function and province of the law and threatens the integrity of judgments that are the basis of the legal system. Unlike speech in other contexts, testimony under oath has the formality and gravity necessary to remind the witness that his or her statements will be the basis for official governmental action, action that often affects the rights and liberties of others. Sworn testimony is quite distinct from lies not spoken under oath and simply intended to puff up oneself. Statutes that prohibit falsely representing that one is speaking on behalf of the Government, or that prohibit impersonating a Government officer, also protect the integrity of Government processes, quite apart from merely restricting false speech. [These] examples, to the extent that they implicate fraud or speech integral to criminal conduct, are inapplicable here.

"As our law and tradition show, then, there are instances in which the falsity of speech bears upon whether it is protected. Some false speech may be prohibited even if analogous true speech could not be. This opinion does not imply that any of these targeted prohibitions are somehow vulnerable. But it also rejects the notion that false speech should be in a general category that is presumptively unprotected."

"[T]he Stolen Valor Act], by its plain terms applies to a false statement made at any time, in any place, to any person. It can be assumed that it would not apply to, say, a theatrical performance. Still, the sweeping, quite unprecedented reach of the statute puts it in conflict with the First Amendment. Here the lie was made in a public meeting, but the statute would apply with equal force to personal, whispered conversations within a home. The statute seeks to control and suppress all false statements on this one subject in almost limitless times and settings. And it does so entirely without regard to whether the lie was made for the purpose of material gain.

"Permitting the government to decree this speech to be a criminal offense, whether shouted from the rooftops or made in a barely audible whisper, would endorse government authority to compile a list of subjects about which false statements are punishable. That governmental power has no clear limiting principle. Our constitutional tradition stands against the idea that we need Oceania's Ministry of Truth."

Kennedy, J., concluded that the Stolen Valor Act could not meet the exacting scrutiny required. He did not question that the statute attempted to further a compelling interest, but he denied that the statute was "actually necessary" to achieve it: "The Government points to no evidence to support its claim that the public's general perception of military awards is diluted by false claims such as those made by Alvarez. [Moreover,] the Government has not shown, and cannot show, why counterspeech would not suffice to achieve its interest. The facts of this case indicate that the dynamics of free speech, of counterspeech, of refutation, can overcome the lie. Respondent lied at a public meeting. Even before the FBI began investigating him for his false statements 'Alvarez was perceived as a phony,' [H]e was ridiculed online [and] his actions were reported in the press. [There] is good reason to believe that a similar fate would befall other false claimants. * * *

"The American people do not need the assistance of a government prosecution to express their high regard for the special place that military heroes hold in our tradition. Only a weak society needs government protection or intervention before it pursues its resolve to preserve the truth. Truth needs neither handcuffs nor a badge for its vindication."

Breyer, J., joined by Kagan, J., concurring in the judgment, departed from the approach taken in *Stevens*: "In determining whether a statute violates the First Amendment, this Court has often found it appropriate to examine the fit between statutory ends and means. In doing so, it has examined speech-related harms, justifications, and potential alternatives. In particular, it has taken account of the seriousness of the speech-related harm the provision will likely cause, the nature and importance of the provision's countervailing objectives, the extent to which the provision will tend to achieve those objectives, and whether there are other, less restrictive ways of doing so. Ultimately the Court has had to determine whether the statute works speech-related harm that is out of proportion to its justifications.

"Sometimes the Court has referred to this approach as 'intermediate scrutiny,' sometimes as 'proportionality' review, sometimes as an examination of 'fit,' and sometimes it has avoided the application of any label at all. Regardless of the label, some such approach is necessary if the First Amendment is to offer proper protection in the many instances in which a statute adversely affects constitutionally protected interests but warrants neither near-automatic condemnation (as 'strict scrutiny' implies) nor near-automatic approval (as is implicit in 'rational basis' review). But in this case, the Court's term 'intermediate scrutiny' describes what I think we should do.

"As the dissent points out, 'there are broad areas in which any attempt by the state to penalize purportedly false speech would present a grave and unacceptable danger of suppressing truthful speech.' Laws restricting false statements about philosophy, religion, history, the social sciences, the arts, and the like raise such concerns, and in many contexts have called for strict scrutiny. But this case does not involve such a law. The dangers of suppressing valuable ideas are lower where, as here, the regulations concern false statements about easily verifiable facts that do not concern such subject matter. Such false factual statements are less likely than are true factual statements to make a valuable contribution to the marketplace of ideas. And the government often has good reasons to prohibit such false speech. But its regulation can nonetheless threaten speech-related harms. * * *

"I must concede, as the Government points out, that this Court has frequently said or implied that false factual statements enjoy little First Amendment protection. But these judicial statements cannot be read to mean 'no protection at all.' False factual statements can serve useful human objectives, for example: in social contexts, where they may prevent embarrassment, protect privacy, shield a person from prejudice, provide the sick with comfort, or preserve a child's innocence; in public contexts, where they may stop a panic or otherwise preserve calm in the face of danger; and even in technical, philosophical, and scientific contexts, where (as Socrates' methods suggest) examination of a false statement (even if made deliberately to mislead) can promote a form of thought that ultimately helps realize the truth. Moreover, as the Court has often said, the threat of criminal prosecution for making a false statement can inhibit the speaker from making true statements, thereby 'chilling' a kind of speech that lies at the First Amendment's heart. * * *

"Further, the pervasiveness of false statements, made for better or for worse motives, made thoughtlessly or deliberately, made with or without accompanying harm, provides a weapon to a government broadly empowered to prosecute falsity without more. And those who are unpopular may fear that the government will use that weapon selectively, say by prosecuting a pacifist who supports his cause by (falsely) claiming to have been a war hero, while ignoring members of other political groups who might make similar false claims.

"I also must concede that many statutes and common law doctrines make the utterance of certain kinds of false statements unlawful. Those prohibitions, however, tend to be narrower than the statute before us, in that they limit the scope of their application, sometimes by requiring proof of specific harm to identifiable victims; sometimes by specifying that the lies be made in contexts in which a tangible harm to others is especially likely to occur; and sometimes by limiting the prohibited lies to those that are particularly likely to produce harm."

Breyer, J., proceeded to argue that this was true of fraud, defamation, the intentional infliction of emotional distress, perjury, materially false statements made to federal officials, false claims of terrorist attacks, impersonation of government officials, and trademark infringements: "While this list is not exhaustive, it is sufficient to show that few statutes, if any, simply prohibit without limitation the telling of a lie, even a lie about one particular matter.

"Instead, in virtually all these instances limitations of context, requirements of proof of injury, and the like, narrow the statute to a subset of lies where specific harm is more likely to occur. The limitations help to make certain that the statute does not allow its threat of liability or criminal punishment to roam at large, discouraging or forbidding the telling of the lie in contexts where harm is unlikely or the need for the prohibition is small.

"The statute before us lacks any such limiting features. It may be construed to prohibit only knowing and intentional acts of deception about readily verifiable facts within the personal knowledge of the speaker, thus reducing the risk that valuable speech is chilled. But it still ranges very broadly. And that breadth means that it creates a significant risk of First Amendment harm. As written, it applies in family, social, or other private contexts, where lies will often cause little harm. It also applies in political contexts, where although such lies are more likely to cause harm, the risk of censorious selectivity by prosecutors is also high. Further, given the potential haziness of individual memory along with the large number of military awards covered (ranging from medals for rifle marksmanship to the Congressional Medal of Honor), there remains a risk of chilling that is not completely eliminated by mens rea requirements; a speaker might still be worried about being prosecuted for a careless false statement, even if he does not have the intent required to render him liable. And so the prohibition may be applied where it should not be applied, for example, to bar stool braggadocio or, in the political arena, subtly but selectively to speakers that the Government does not like. * * *

"[I]t should be possible significantly to diminish or eliminate these remaining risks by enacting a similar but more finely tailored statute. For example, not all military awards are alike. Congress might determine that some warrant greater protection than others. And a more finely tailored statute might, as other kinds of statutes prohibiting false factual statements have done, insist upon a showing that the false statement caused specific harm or at least was material, or focus its coverage on lies most likely to be harmful or on contexts where such lies are most likely to cause harm. I recognize that in some contexts, particularly political contexts, such a narrowing will not always be easy to achieve. In the political arena a false statement is more likely to make a behavioral difference (say, by leading the listeners to vote for the speaker) but at the same time criminal prosecution is particularly dangerous (say, by radically changing a potential election result) and consequently can more easily result in censorship of speakers and their [ideas.] I would also note, like the plurality, that in this area more accurate information will normally counteract the lie. And an accurate, publicly available register of military awards, easily obtainable by political opponents, may well adequately protect the integrity of an award against those who would falsely claim to have earned it. And so it is likely that a more narrowly tailored statute combined with such information-disseminating devices will effectively serve Congress' end.

"The Government has provided no convincing explanation as to why a more finely tailored statute would not work. [That] being so, I find the statute as presently drafted works disproportionate constitutional harm. It consequently fails intermediate scrutiny, and so violates the First Amendment."

ALITO, J., joined by Scalia and Thomas, JJ., dissenting, also departed from the *Stevens* approach: "Time and again, this Court has recognized that as a general matter false factual statements possess no intrinsic First Amendment value. Consistent with this recognition, many kinds of false factual statements have long been proscribed without 'rais[ing] any Constitutional problem.' Laws prohibiting fraud, perjury, and defamation, for example, were in existence when the First Amendment was adopted, and their constitutionality is now beyond question. We have also described as falling outside the First Amendment's protective shield certain false factual statements that were neither illegal nor tortious at the time of the Amendment's adoption. The right to freedom of speech has been held to permit recovery for the intentional infliction of emotional distress by means of a false statement. And in *Hill*, the Court concluded that the free speech right allows recovery for the even more modern tort of false-light invasion of privacy.

"In line with these holdings, it has long been assumed that the First Amendment is not offended by prominent criminal statutes with no close common-law analog. The most well known of these is probably 18 U.S.C. § 1001. [Unlike] perjury, § 1001 is not limited to statements made under oath or before an official government tribunal. Nor does it require any showing of 'pecuniary or property loss to the government.' Instead, the statute is based on the need to protect 'agencies from the perversion which *might* result from the deceptive practices described.'

"Still other statutes make it a crime to falsely represent that one is speaking on behalf of, or with the approval of, the Federal Government. We have recognized that § 912, like § 1001, does not require a showing of pecuniary or property loss and that its purpose is to 'maintain the general good repute and dignity' of Government service. All told, there are more than 100 federal criminal statutes that punish false statements made in connection with areas of federal agency concern. These examples amply demonstrate that false statements of fact merit no First Amendment protection in their own right. It is true, as Justice Breyer notes, that many in our society either approve or condone certain discrete categories of false statements, including false statements made to prevent harm to innocent victims and so-called 'white lies.' But respondent's false claim to have received the Medal of Honor did not fall into any of these categories. His lie did not 'prevent embarrassment, protect privacy, shield a person from prejudice, provide the sick with comfort, or preserve a child's innocence.' Nor did his lie 'stop a panic or otherwise preserve calm in the face of danger' or further philosophical or scientific debate. Respondent's claim, like all those covered by the Stolen Valor Act, served no valid purpose. [The] lies covered by the Stolen Valor Act have no intrinsic value and thus merit no First Amendment protection unless their prohibition would chill other expression that falls within the Amendment's scope. * * *

"[T]here are broad areas in which any attempt by the state to penalize purportedly false speech would present a grave and unacceptable danger of suppressing truthful speech. Laws restricting false statements about philosophy, religion, history, the social sciences, the arts, and other matters of public concern would present such a threat. The point is not that there is no such thing as truth or falsity in these areas or that the truth is always impossible to ascertain, but rather that it is perilous to permit the state to be the arbiter of truth. * * *

"In stark contrast to hypothetical laws prohibiting false statements about history, science, and similar matters, the Stolen Valor Act presents no risk at all that valuable speech will be suppressed. The speech punished by the Act is not only verifiably false and entirely lacking in intrinsic value, but it also fails to serve any instrumental purpose that the First Amendment might protect. Tellingly, when asked at oral argument what truthful speech the Stolen Valor Act might chill, even respondent's counsel conceded that the answer is none.

"Neither of the two opinions endorsed by Justices in the majority claims that the false statements covered by the Stolen Valor Act possess either intrinsic or instrumental value. Instead, those opinions appear to be based on the distinct concern that the Act suffers from overbreadth." Alito, J., referred to the plurality's concern about "personal, whispered conversations within a home") and Breyer, J.'s argument that the Act "applies in family, social, or other private contexts" and in "political contexts." But, Alito, J., argued that "to strike down a statute on the basis that it is overbroad, it is necessary to show that the statute's 'overbreadth [is] substantial, not only in an absolute sense, but also relative to [its] plainly legitimate sweep.' The plurality and the concurrence do not even attempt to make this showing. The plurality additionally worries that a decision sustaining the Stolen Valor Act might prompt Congress and the state legislatures to enact laws criminalizing lies about 'an endless list of subjects.' The plurality apparently fears that we will see laws making it a crime to lie about civilian awards such as college degrees or certificates of achievement in the arts and sports.

"This concern is likely unfounded. With very good reason, military honors have traditionally been regarded as quite different from civilian awards. Nearly a century ago, Congress made it a crime to wear a military medal without authorization; we have no comparable tradition regarding such things as Super Bowl rings, Oscars, or Phi Beta Kappa keys. In any event, if the plurality's concern is not entirely fanciful, it falls outside the purview of the First Amendment. The problem that the plurality foresees—that legislative bodies will enact unnecessary and overly intrusive criminal laws—applies regardless of whether the laws in question involve speech or nonexpressive conduct. If there is a problem with, let us say, a law making it a criminal offense to falsely claim to have been a high school valedictorian, the problem is not the suppression of speech but the misuse of the criminal law, which should be reserved for conduct that inflicts or threatens truly serious societal harm. The objection to this hypothetical law would be the same as the objection to a law making it a crime to eat potato chips during the graduation ceremony at which the high school valedictorian is recognized. The safeguard against such laws is democracy, not the First Amendment. Not every foolish law is unconstitutional. * * *

"The Stolen Valor Act is a narrow law enacted to address an important problem, and it presents no threat to freedom of expression. I would sustain the constitutionality of the Act, and I therefore respectfully dissent."

SECTION 3. IS SOME PROTECTED SPEECH LESS EQUAL THAN OTHER PROTECTED SPEECH?

II. COMMERCIAL SPEECH

P. 889, after note 5

6.   In the absence of the consent of physicians, Vermont prohibits pharmacists from selling information about the drugs physicians prescribe to pharmaceutical companies or to those who provide reports to such companies for marketing purposes. Pharmacists, on the other hand, are permitted to sell to private or academic researchers even without consent. Is the sale of such information to pharmaceutical companies commercial speech? If not, does it burden commercial speech in a way that should trigger heightened scrutiny? Should protection of physician privacy be sufficient to justify the statute? See *Sorrell v. IMS Health Inc.,* 131 S.Ct. 2653 (2011).

SECTION 7. GOVERNMENT SUPPORT OF SPEECH

I. SUBSIDIES OF SPEECH

P. 1022, add as footnote cc, at the end 1st full para.

cc Accordingly, the Court, per Roberts, C.J., ruled that a program funding nongovernmental organizations to combat HIV/AIDS worldwide could not require recipients to adopt or maintain a policy explicitly opposing prostitution. Because the condition applied to speech that was not within the scope of the federal program, it unconstitutionally burdened the First Amendment rights of the recipients. *Agency for Intern. Dev. v. Alliance for Open Society Intern., Inc.*, 133 S.Ct. 2321 (2013). Scalia and Thomas, JJ., dissented. Kagan, J., did not participate.

III. GOVERNMENT AS EMPLOYER

P. 1048, add to footnote a

Bureau of Duryea v. Guarnieri, 131 S.Ct. 2488 (2011), held that retaliation against a public employee for seeking redress in the courts would be subject to *Pickering* standards whether the law suit was framed as a violation of freedom of speech or as a right to petition the government for redress of grievances. If the matter relates to private speech, no redress is available. If the matter relates to public speech, *Pickering* is applicable.

SECTION 8. THE ELECTRONIC MEDIA

II. THE ELECTRONIC MEDIA AND CONTENT REGULATION

P. 1089, add at end of note 3

In distinguishing the facts of *Cohen,* for many years the FCC had interpreted *Pacifica* to require the dwelling upon or repeating at length descriptions of sexual or excretory organs or activities. In 2004 and 2006, however, the agency determined that fleeting expletives or partial nudity could meet the offensiveness requirement for an indecency finding. FCC V. FOX TELEVISION STATIONS, INC. II, 132 S. Ct. 2307 (2012), avoided confronting the question whether the fleeting expletives policy violated the First Amendment by holding that Fox, which had aired award shows in 2002 and 2003 in which Cher and Nicole Richie had used swear words and ABC, which had aired an NYPD Blue episode with 7 seconds of partial nudity, had not been afforded proper notice of the FCC policy. The Court, per KENNEDY, J., concluded that the policy was unconstitutionally vague under the Due Process Clause with regard to these incidents and left its assessment of the policy as applied to those with adequate notice for another day.

SECTION 9. THE RIGHT NOT TO SPEAK, THE RIGHT TO ASSOCIATE, AND THE RIGHT NOT TO ASSOCIATE

I. THE RIGHT NOT TO BE ASSOCIATED WITH PARTICULAR IDEAS

P. 1109, substitute for 1st paragraph of note 8

8. ***Compelled monetary subsidies.*** (a) A series of cases have invalidated government forced monetary contributions for support of speech opposed by the contributors. *Abood v. Detroit Bd. of Educ.*, 431 U.S. 209 (1977), held that members of a public employee bargaining unit who are not members of the union can be compelled to pay a service fee to the union for its collective bargaining expenses (because they would otherwise be free riders and that would endanger labor peace and because of the importance of stable unions), but they may not be charged for political expenses if they object to the use of union funds supporting political candidates or political views. Similarly, *Keller v. State Bar of California*, 496 U.S. 1 (1990), held that the use of compulsory dues to finance political and ideological activities with which members disagreed violated their First Amendment right of free speech when such expenditures were not necessarily or reasonably incurred for purpose of regulating the legal profession or improving quality of legal services.[k] *International Ass'n of Machinists v. Street,* 367 U.S. 740 (1961), held that "dissent is not to be presumed" and that only employees who have affirmatively made known to the union their opposition to political uses of their funds are entitled to relief for political expenditures. *Chicago Teachers v. Hudson*, 475 U.S. 292 (1986), spoke to the process for determining which part of the fees were germane to collective bargaining and which was political, holding that "constitutional requirements for the Union's collection of agency fees include an adequate explanation of the basis for the fee, a reasonably prompt opportunity to challenge the amount of the fee before an impartial decisionmaker, and an escrow for the amounts reasonably in dispute while such challenges are pending."

KNOX v. SERVICE EMPLOYEES INT'L UNION, 132 S.Ct. 2277 (2012), per ALITO, J., held that unions that have a special assessment for political purposes must issue a *Hudson* notice and may not exact funds from non-union members of a bargaining unit without their affirmative consent. In lengthy dicta, Alito, J., suggested that the practice of requiring non-members to opt out of supporting political expenditures authorized by *Hudson*, may not

---

[k] But *Board of Regents v. Southworth*, 529 U.S. 217 (2000), also held that despite ideological objections, compulsory exactions might be justified by the strength of the governmental interest. It decreed that no refund of student fees was appropriate so long as allocation of funding was viewpoint neutral on the ground that the interest in stimulating diverse ideas on campus outweighed the interests of objecting students. Is the First Amendment objection mistaken because "the mere act of paying a mandatory assessment does not identify the payer with the same message her payments help fund"? Gregory Klass, *The Very Idea of a First Amendment Right Against Compelled Subsidization*, 38 U.C.Davis L. Rev. 1087, 1116–1117 (2005).

only be statutorily changed to an opt in requirement as was held in *Davenport v. Washington Educ. Ass'n*, 551 U.S. 177 (2007), but may be required under the First Amendment even when the dues assessment is not special. In further dicta, Alito, J., argued that the free rider argument for requiring non-members to pay a service fee to the unions who are required to represent them is an "anomaly." He did not discuss the merits of the argument that the service fee requirement is necessary to assure labor stability and peace.

SOTOMAYOR, J., joined by Ginsburg, J., concurred in the judgment. She agreed that non-members should not be compelled to provide financial support for political expenditures they oppose, but argued that the opt-in remedy was not argued by either party, and was outside the briefs and the scope of the questions presented.[1]

(b) *United States v. United Foods, Inc.*, 533 U.S. 405 (2001) held that objecting mushroom handlers cannot be compelled to fund generic advertisements supporting mushroom sales.[II] Nonetheless, taxpayers routinely fund speech activities to which they are opposed without First Amendment rights being violated.

SECTION 10.   WEALTH AND THE POLITICAL PROCESS: CONCERNS FOR EQUALITY

P. 1133, add footnote at end of 1st full paragraph

Although restrictions on political speech are subject to First Amendment scrutiny, *Nevada Commission on Ethics v. Corrigan*, 131 S.Ct. 2343 (2011), held that legislative recusal rules did not impermissibly restrict the First Amendment rights of legislators. Indeed, the Court maintained generally that restrictions on legislators' voting are not restrictions upon legislators' protected speech.

P. 1134, add to end of footnote e

Arizona Free Enterprise Clubs Freedom Club PAC v. Bennett, 131 S.Ct. 2806 (2011), extended *Davis*, invalidating an Arizona scheme in which candidates who accepted public financing in exchange for foregoing private contributions were receiving matching funds virtually dollar for dollar when their opponents in conjunction with their independent supporters spent beyond the public financing cap.

P. 1149, add at end of fn. b

American Tradition Partnership, Inc. v. Bullock, 132 S.Ct. 2490 (2012), summarily reaffirmed *Citizens United* and rejected the argument that a long history of corruption in Montana served to distinguish that precedent.

---

[1]   Breyer, J., joined by Kagan, J., dissenting, agreed with Sotomayor, J., but argued that nonmembers would not in fact over the course of the year be forced to support political expenditures they opposed because the percentage of their dues would not exceed the percentage used for collective bargaining purposes and even if it did the system authorized by *Hudson* would assure that they would eventually be protected.

[II]   But see *Glickman v. Wileman Bros. & Elliott, Inc.*, 521 U.S. 457 (1997) (tree fruit producers can be compelled to pay assessments for advertising). Can *United Foods* be reconciled with *Zauderer*? For doubts, see Robert Post, *Transparent and Efficient Markets*, 40 Val.U.L.Rev. 555 (2006).

CHAPTER 8

FREEDOM OF RELIGION

∎ ∎ ∎

SECTION 1. ESTABLISHMENT CLAUSE

IV. OFFICIAL ACKNOWLEDGMENT OF RELIGION

P. 1221, add fn. at end of last full ¶

a. See also Thomas, J., dissenting from the denial of certiorari in *Utah Highway Control Ass'n v. American Atheists, Inc.*, 132 S.Ct. 12 (2011), in which the Tenth Circuit held violative of the Establishment Clause the private association's "commemorating officers who died in the line of duty by placing memorials, in the form of 12–by 6–foot white crosses, at or near locations where the officers were killed": "Our jurisprudence provides no principled basis by which a lower court could discern whether *Lemon*/endorsement, or some other test, should apply" because "both tests are so utterly indeterminate."

SECTION 2. FREE EXERCISE CLAUSE AND RELATED PROBLEMS

I. CONFLICT WITH STATE REGULATION

P. 1263, before II

4. ***Choosing a "minister."*** In HOSANNA–TABOR EVANGELICAL LUTHERAN CHURCH AND SCHOOL v. EQUAL EMPLOYMENT OPPORTUNITY COMM'N, 132 S.Ct. 694 (2012), after the church school terminated Cheryl Perich, a teacher who had completed the church's academic requirements to become a "minister," she filed a claim with the EEOC that her termination violated the Americans with Disabilities Act. Although "the Courts of Appeals have uniformly recognized [the] existence of a ministerial exception barring certain employment discrimination claims against religious institutions—an exception 'rooted in the First Amendment's guarantees of religious freedom,' " the Sixth Circuit concluded that Perich "did not qualify as a 'minister' under the exception." A unanimous Court, per ROBERTS, J., reversed: "The Establishment Clause prevents the Government from appointing ministers, and the Free Exercise Clause prevents it from interfering with the freedom of religious groups to select their [own] who will personify its beliefs."

The Court was "reluctant [to] adopt a rigid formula for deciding when an employee qualifies as a minister," but noted that the church "held Perich out as a minister, with a role distinct from that of most of its members," and that she "held herself out as a minister of the church" in various ways. "Perich's title as a minister reflected a significant degree of religious training followed by a formal process of commissioning. [S]he had to pass an oral examination by a faculty committee at a Lutheran college. It took Perich six years to fulfill these requirements. [She] taught her students religion four days a week, and led them in prayer three times a day. Once a week, she took her students to a school-wide chapel service, and—about twice a year—she took her turn leading [it.]" Finally, in regarding "the relative amount of time Perich spent performing religious functions as largely determinative" (this "consumed only 45 minutes of each workday") rather than just "relevant," the Sixth Circuit "gave too much weight to the fact that lay teachers at the school performed the same religious duties. [The] heads of congregations themselves often have a mix of duties, including secular ones such as helping to manage the congregations' finances, supervising purely secular personnel, and overseeing the upkeep of facilities."

ALITO, J., joined by Kagan, J., concurred, urging that "courts should focus on the function performed by persons who work for religious bodies. [The] 'ministerial' exception [should] apply to any 'employee' who leads a religious organization, conducts worship services or important religious ceremonies or rituals, or serves as a messenger or teacher of its faith."[c]

---

[c] Thomas, J., concurred, adding that the fact that the church "sincerely considered Perich a minister" was sufficient for him to apply the ministerial exception.

CHAPTER 9

EQUAL PROTECTION

■ ■ ■

SECTION 1. TRADITIONAL APPROACH

P. 1308, add after top paragraph

ARMOUR v. INDIANAPOLIS, 132 S.Ct. 2073 (2012), per BREYER, J., rejected an equal protection challenge to a city's policy for apportioning the costs of sewer construction. Under its initial financing scheme, Indianapolis billed property owners who wished to be hooked up to a sewer line $9,278 each, payable either in one lump sum or in installments spread over as many as 30 years. Very shortly thereafter, but after some property owners had paid in full, the city switched to a new financing system and decided to forgive the debts of those paying on the installment plan. It refused, however, to provide refunds to those who had paid upfront. As a result, some property owners paid as little as $309 while others paid $9,278. The Court ruled that considerations of administrative convenience provided a rational basis for the city's policy of forgiving unpaid assessments but not refunding any money already paid. After switching financing schemes, to continue "unpaid-debt collection could have proved complex and expensive," and "[t]o have added refunds to forgiveness" would have produced the "administrative costs [of] processing refunds" for a multitude of projects. The Court declined to find that the city had another rational basis in avoiding the "fiscal challenge" of paying refunds Nevertheless, it noted that the city could not just issue checks to every complaining party "without taking funding from other programs or finding additional revenue," adding that if "the City had tried to keep the amount of revenue it lost constant (a rational goal) but spread it evenly among the apparently thousands of homeowners involved in any of the [projects for which assessments had initially been made under the old system, with some property owners paying upfront and others in installments], the result would have been yet smaller individual payments, even more likely to have been too small to justify the administrative expense."

ROBERTS, C.J., joined by Scalia and Alito, JJ., dissented, emphasizing that the Indiana law that authorized the apportionment of sewer costs among property owners required at least roughly equal apportionment: "We have never before held that administrative burdens justify grossly disparate tax treatment of those the State has provided should be treated alike." Because "[t]he Equal Protection Clause is concerned [only] with 'gross' disparity in taxing," the Chief Justice would not have required refunds to owners who had paid upfront for hook-ups to other lines if other owners' installment payments over a period of years had produced less egregious inequalities. He added: "The Court is willing to concede that 'administrative considerations could not justify [an] unfair system' in which 'a city arbitrarily allocate[s] taxes among a few citizens while forgiving many others on the ground that it is cheaper and easier to collect taxes from a few people than from many.' [If] the quoted language does not accurately describe this case, I am not sure what it would reach."

SECTION 2. RACE AND ETHNIC ANCESTRY

IV. AFFIRMATIVE ACTION

P. 1399, after note 5

FISHER V. UNIVERSITY OF TEXAS
___ U.S. ___, 133 S.Ct. 2411, ___ L.Ed.2d ___ (2013).

JUSTICE KENNEDY delivered the opinion of the Court.

[Abigail Fisher, a Caucasian who was denied admission to the University of Texas, brought suit, challenging the University's use of race in its admissions process. The University's admissions policy had a complex history. Before 1997, the University "considered two factors: a numerical score reflecting an applicant's" test scores and high school grades (Academic Index or AI) and the applicant's race. After a lower court held that any consideration of race was unconstitutional, the University replaced the race-based component of its process with a Personal Achievement Index (PAI), reflecting such considerations as leadership, work experience, extra-curricular activities, and "special circumstances" including "growing up in a single-parent home, speaking a language other than English at home, [and] the socioeconomic condition of the student's family." At about the same time, the Texas Legislature adopted a Top Ten Percent Law that "grants automatic admission to [all] students in the top 10% of their class at high schools in Texas that comply with certain standards." Roughly three-quarters of the University's students gain admission under the Top Ten Percent formula. In the last year that the University admitted part of its class based on a formula that combined AI and race-blind PAI scores, while admitting its other students under the Top Ten Percent Plan, the entering class was 4.5% African-American and 16.9 percent Hispanic, in comparison with 4.1% and 14.5% in the last year in which the University took race into account.

[Following the 2003 decision in *Grutter v. Bollinger*, the University resumed making race a consideration in its admissions process, this time as an express factor in computing the PAI that it continued to use for applicants who were not admitted pursuant to the Top Ten Percent Plan. "Race [was] not assigned an explicit numerical value, but it is undisputed that race [was] a meaningful factor." The internal document expressing the University's decision to inquire into race as part of its admission process "relied in substantial part on a study of a subset of undergraduate classes containing between 5 and 24 students," few of which "had substantial enrollment" by racial minorities. It "concluded that the University lacked a 'critical mass' of minority students." In challenging the University's reliance on race in computing applicants' PAI, Fisher did not attack any other element of the admissions process, including the Top Ten Percent Plan. Nor did she ask the Court to overrule *Grutter*, which she argued that the lower courts had misapplied when they ruled against her.]

Grutter made clear that racial "classifications are constitutional only if they are narrowly tailored to further compelling governmental interests." And *Grutter* endorsed Justice Powell's conclusion in *Bakke* that "the attainment of a diverse student body . . . is a constitutionally permissible goal for an institution of higher education." [According] to *Grutter*, a university's "educational judgment that such diversity is essential to its educational mission is one to which we defer." [The] District Court and Court of Appeals were thus correct in finding that *Grutter* calls for deference to the University's conclusion that a diverse student body would serve its educational goals. There is disagreement about whether *Grutter* was consistent with the principles of equal protection in approving this compelling interest in diversity. See [opinions in this case] (Scalia, J., concurring); (Thomas, J., concurring); (Ginsburg, J., dissenting). But the parties here do not ask the Court to revisit that aspect of *Grutter*'s holding.

[Once] the University has established that its goal of diversity is consistent with strict scrutiny, [the] University must prove that [its] means are narrowly tailored to that goal. On this point, the University receives no deference. [I]t remains at all times the University's obligation to demonstrate, and the Judiciary's obligation to determine, that admissions processes "ensure that each applicant is evaluated as an individual and not in a way that makes an applicant's race or ethnicity the defining feature of his or her application." Narrow tailoring also requires that the reviewing court verify that it is "necessary" for a university to use race to achieve the educational benefits of diversity. Although "[n]arrow tailoring does not require exhaustion of every *conceivable* race-neutral alternative," [strict] scrutiny imposes on the university the ultimate burden of demonstrating [that] available, workable race-neutral alternatives do not suffice.

Rather than perform this searching examination, [the] Court of Appeals held petitioner could challenge only "whether [the University's] decision to reintroduce race as a factor in admissions was made in good faith." [It further] ruled that to "second-guess the merits" of this aspect of the University's decision was a task it was "ill-equipped to perform" and that it would attempt only to "ensure that [the University's] decision to adopt a race-conscious admissions policy followed from [a process of] good faith consideration." The Court of Appeals thus concluded that "the narrow-tailoring inquiry—like the compelling-interest inquiry—is undertaken with a degree of deference to the Universit[y]." These expressions of the controlling standard are at odds with *Grutter*'s command that "all racial classifications imposed by government 'must be analyzed by a reviewing court under strict scrutiny.'" [Strict] scrutiny does not permit a court to accept a school's assertion that its admissions process uses race in a permissible way without a court giving close analysis to the evidence of how the process works in practice.

[Strict] scrutiny must not be "strict in theory, but fatal in fact." But the opposite is also true. Strict scrutiny must not be strict in theory but feeble in fact. [The] judgment of the Court of Appeals is vacated, and the case is remanded for further proceedings consistent with this opinion.

JUSTICE SCALIA, concurring.

I adhere to the view I expressed in *Grutter* that "The Constitution proscribes government discrimination on the basis of race, and state-provided education is no exception." [But because t]he petitioner in this case did not ask us to overrule *Grutter,* [I] join the Court's opinion in full.

JUSTICE THOMAS, concurring.

[Our] desegregation cases establish that the Constitution prohibits public schools from discriminating based on race, even if discrimination is necessary to the schools' survival. [It] follows, a fortiori, that the putative educational benefits of student body diversity cannot justify racial discrimination: If a State does not have a compelling interest in the *existence* of a university, it certainly cannot have a compelling interest in the supposed benefits that might accrue to that university from racial discrimination.

My view of the Constitution is the one advanced by the plaintiffs in *Brown*: "[N]o State has any authority under the equal-protection clause of the Fourteenth Amendment to use race as a factor in affording educational opportunities among its citizens." [This] principle is neither new nor difficult to understand. In 1868, decades before *Plessy*, the Iowa Supreme Court held that schools may not discriminate against applicants based on their skin color. In *Clark* v. *Board of Directors*, 24 Iowa 266 (1868), a school denied admission to a student because she was black, and "public sentiment [was] opposed to the intermingling of white and colored children in the same schools." The Iowa Supreme Court rejected that flimsy justification, holding that "all the youths are equal before the law, and there is no discretion vested in the board . . . or elsewhere, to interfere with or disturb that equality."[a]

[The] worst forms of racial discrimination in this Nation have always been accompanied by straight-faced representations that discrimination helped minorities. Slaveholders argued that slavery was a "positive good" that civilized blacks and elevated them in every dimension of life. [A] century later, segregationists similarly asserted [that] separate schools protected black children from racist white students and teachers. [The] University's discrimination "stamp[s] [blacks and Hispanics] with a badge of inferiority." [Although] most blacks and Hispanics attending the University were admitted without discrimination under the Top Ten Percent plan [no] one can distinguish those students from the ones whose race played a role in their admission.

JUSTICE GINSBURG, dissenting.

The University [is] endeavoring [to] achieve student-body diversity through an admissions policy patterned after the Harvard plan referenced as exemplary in Justice Powell's opinion in *Bakke*. And, like so many educational institutions across the Nation, the University has taken care to follow the model approved by the Court in *Grutter*. Petitioner urges that Texas' Top Ten Percent Law and race-blind holistic review of each application achieve significant diversity, so the University must be content with those alternatives. I have said before and reiterate here that only an ostrich could regard the supposedly neutral alternatives as race unconscious. Texas' percentage plan was adopted with racially segregated neighborhoods and schools front and center stage. It is race consciousness, not blindness to race, that drives such plans. As for holistic review, if universities cannot explicitly include race as a factor, many may "resort to camouflage" to "maintain their minority enrollment."

[Because] the University's admissions policy [satisfies the standards set out in] Justice Powell's opinion in *Bakke* and the Court's decision in *Grutter,* [I] would affirm the judgment of the Court of Appeals.[b]

---

[a] The decision was based on Iowa law, not the Fourteenth Amendment.

[b] Kagan, J., did not participate.

SECTION 4. SPECIAL SCRUTINY FOR OTHER CLASSIFICATIONS: DOCTRINE AND DEBATES

I. SEXUAL ORIENTATION

P. 1471, after note 6

UNITED STATES V. WINDSOR
__ U.S. __, 133 S.Ct. 2675, ___ L.Ed.2d ___ (2013).

JUSTICE KENNEDY delivered the opinion of the Court.

In 1996, as some States were beginning to consider the concept of same-sex marriage, and before any State had acted to permit it, Congress enacted the Defense of Marriage Act (DOMA). [Section] 2, which has not been challenged here, allows States to refuse to recognize same-sex marriages performed under the laws of other States. Section 3 [provides that in] "determining the meaning of any Act of Congress [or other provision of federal law], the word 'marriage' means only a legal union between one man and one woman as husband and wife, and the word 'spouse' refers only to a person of the opposite sex who is a husband or a wife." The definitional provision does not [forbid] States from enacting laws permitting same-sex marriages [but it] does control over 1,000 federal laws in which marital or spousal status is addressed as a matter of federal law.

Edith Windsor and Thea Spyer [were a single-sex New York couple who got married in Canada and whose marriage the] State of New York deems to be a valid one. Spyer died in February 2009, and left her entire estate to Windsor. Because DOMA denies federal recognition to same-sex spouses, Windsor did not qualify for the marital exemption from the federal estate tax. [She] paid $363,053 in estate taxes and [brought suit arguing that DOMA violated her equal protection rights by denying her treatment as] a "surviving spouse."

[Until] recent years, many citizens had not even considered the possibility that two persons of the same sex might aspire to occupy the same status and dignity as that of a man and woman in lawful marriage. [But the] limitation of lawful marriage to heterosexual couples, which for centuries had been deemed both necessary and fundamental, came to be seen in New York and certain other States as an unjust exclusion. [By] history and tradition the definition and regulation of marriage [has] been treated as being within the authority and realm of the separate States. Yet it is further established that Congress, in enacting discrete statutes, can make determinations that bear on marital rights and privileges. [For example,] in establishing income-based criteria for Social Security benefits, Congress decided that although state law would determine in general who qualifies as an applicant's spouse, common-law marriages also should be recognized, regardless of any particular State's view on these relationships.

Though th[is and other] examples establish the constitutionality of limited federal laws that regulate the meaning of marriage in order to further federal policy, DOMA has a far greater reach. And its operation is directed to a class of persons that the laws of New York, and of 11 other States, have sought to protect. [DOMA] rejects the long established precept that the incidents, benefits, and obligations of marriage are uniform for all married couples within each State, though they may vary, subject to constitutional guarantees, from one State to the next. Despite these considerations, it is unnecessary to decide whether this federal intrusion on state power is a violation of the Constitution because it disrupts the federal balance. The State's power in defining the marital relation is of central relevance in this case quite apart from principles of federalism. Here the State's decision to give this class of persons the right to marry conferred upon them a dignity and status of immense import. When the State used its historic and essential authority to define the marital relation in this way, its role and its power in making the decision enhanced the recognition, dignity, and protection of the class in their own community. DOMA, because of its reach and extent, departs from this history and tradition of reliance on state law to define marriage. " '[D]iscriminations of an unusual character especially suggest careful consideration to determine whether they are obnoxious to the constitutional provision.' " *Romer*.

[DOMA] seeks to injure the very class New York seeks to protect. By doing so it violates basic due process and equal protection principles applicable to the Federal Government. See U. S. Const., Amdt. 5; *Bolling* v. *Sharpe*. The Constitution's guarantee of equality "must at the very least mean that a bare congressional desire to harm a politically unpopular group cannot" justify disparate treatment of that group. In determining whether a law is motivated by an improper animus or purpose, "[d]iscriminations of an unusual character" especially require careful consideration. DOMA cannot survive under these principles. DOMA's unusual deviation from the usual tradition of recognizing and accepting state definitions of marriage here operates to deprive same-sex couples of the benefits and responsibilities that come with the federal recognition of their marriages. This is strong evidence of a law having the purpose and effect of disapproval of that class. The avowed purpose and practical effect of the law here in question are to impose a disadvantage, a separate status, and so a stigma upon all who enter into same-sex marriages made lawful by the unquestioned authority of the States.

The history of DOMA's enactment and its own text demonstrate that interference with the equal dignity of same-sex marriages [was] more than an incidental effect of the federal statute. It was its essence. The

House [Report] concluded that DOMA expresses "both moral disapproval of homosexuality, and a moral conviction that heterosexuality better comports with traditional (especially Judeo-Christian) morality." The stated purpose of the law was to promote an "interest in protecting the traditional moral teachings reflected in heterosexual-only marriage laws." *Ibid.*

[DOMA's] principal effect is to identify a subset of state sanctioned marriages and make them unequal. The principal purpose is to impose inequality, not for other reasons like governmental efficiency. [DOMA] undermines both the public and private significance of state sanctioned same-sex marriages; for it tells those couples, and all the world, that their otherwise valid marriages are unworthy of federal recognition. This places same-sex couples in an unstable position of being in a second-tier marriage. The differentiation demeans the couple, whose moral and sexual choices the Constitution protects, see *Lawrence*, and whose relationship the State has sought to dignify. And it humiliates tens of thousands of children now being raised by same-sex couples.

[The Court therefore holds that] DOMA is unconstitutional as a deprivation of the liberty of the person protected by the Fifth Amendment of the Constitution. [The] federal statute is invalid, for no legitimate purpose overcomes the purpose and effect to disparage and to injure those whom the State, by its marriage laws, sought to protect in personhood and dignity. By seeking to displace this protection and treating those persons as living in marriages less respected than others, the federal statute is in violation of the Fifth Amendment. This opinion and its holding are confined to those lawful marriages. * * *

CHIEF JUSTICE ROBERTS, dissenting.

Interests in uniformity and stability amply justified Congress's decision to retain the definition of marriage that, at that point, had been adopted by every State in our Nation, and every nation in the world. [That] the Federal Government treated this fundamental question differently than it treated variations over consanguinity or minimum age is hardly surprising—and hardly enough to support a conclusion that the "principal purpose" [of those] who voted for it, and the President who signed it, was a bare desire to harm. Nor do the snippets of legislative history and the banal title of the Act to which the majority points suffice to make such a showing. At least without some more convincing evidence that the Act's principal purpose was to codify malice, and that it furthered *no* legitimate government interests, I would not tar the political branches with the brush of bigotry.

But while I disagree with the result to which the majority's analysis leads it in this case, I think it more important to point out that its analysis leads no further. The Court does not have before it, and the logic of its opinion does not decide, the distinct question whether the States, in the exercise of their "historic and essential authority to define the marital relation," may continue to utilize the traditional definition of marriage. [I] think the majority goes off course, as I have said, but it is undeniable that its judgment is based on federalism. * * *

JUSTICE SCALIA, with whom JUSTICE THOMAS joins, dissenting.

There are many remarkable things about the majority's merits holding. The first is how rootless and shifting its justifications are. For example, the opinion starts with seven full pages about the traditional power of States to define domestic relations[, but] we are eventually told that "it is unnecessary to decide whether this federal intrusion on state power is a violation of the Constitution." [Near] the end of the opinion, we are told that although the "equal protection guarantee of the Fourteenth Amendment makes [the] Fifth Amendment [due process] right all the more specific and all the better understood and preserved"—what can *that* mean?—"the Fifth Amendment itself withdraws from Government the power to degrade or demean in the way this law does." The only possible interpretation of this statement is that the Equal Protection Clause, even the Equal Protection Clause as incorporated in the Due Process Clause, is not the basis for today's holding.

[Moreover], if this is meant to be an equal-protection opinion, it is a confusing one. The opinion does not resolve and indeed does not even mention what had been the central question in this litigation: whether, under the Equal Protection Clause, laws restricting marriage to a man and a woman are reviewed for more than mere rationality. [As] nearly as I can tell, the Court [does] not apply strict scrutiny, and its central propositions are taken from rational-basis cases like *Moreno*. But the Court certainly does not *apply* anything that resembles that deferential framework.

The majority opinion need not get into the strict-vs. rational-basis scrutiny question, and need not justify its holding under either, because it says that DOMA is unconstitutional as "a deprivation of the liberty of the person protected by the Fifth Amendment of the Constitution"; that it violates "basic due process" principles; and that it inflicts an "injury and indignity" of a kind that denies "an essential part of the liberty protected by the Fifth Amendment. The majority never utters the dread words "substantive due process," perhaps sensing the disrepute into which that doctrine has fallen, but that is what those statements mean.

[The] sum of all the Court's nonspecific hand-waving is that this law is invalid because it is motivated by a "bare . . . desire to harm" couples in same-sex marriages. [But] the Constitution does not forbid the government to enforce traditional moral and sexual norms. [Even] setting aside traditional moral disapproval of same-sex marriage (or indeed same-sex sex), there are many perfectly valid—indeed, downright boring—justifying rationales for this legislation. [To] choose just one[,]

DOMA avoids difficult choice-of-law issues that will now arise absent a uniform federal definition of marriage. Imagine a pair of women who marry in Albany and then move to Alabama, which does not "recognize as valid any marriage of parties of the same sex." When the couple files their next federal tax return, may it be a joint one? Which State's law controls, for federal-law purposes: their State of celebration (which recognizes the marriage) or their State of domicile (which does not)? [Further,] DOMA preserves the intended effects of prior legislation against then-unforeseen changes in circumstance. When Congress provided (for example) that a special estate-tax exemption would exist for spouses, this exemption reached only *opposite-sex* spouses—those being the only sort that were recognized in *any* State at the time of DOMA's passage.

[The] Court mentions none of this. Instead, it accuses the Congress that enacted this law and the President who signed it of [having] acted with *malice*—with the *"purpose"* "to disparage and to injure" same-sex couples. * * * I am sure these accusations are quite untrue.

[It] is one thing for a society to elect change; it is another for a court of law to impose change by adjudging those who oppose it *hostes humani generis*, enemies of the human race.

The penultimate sentence of the majority's opinion is a naked declaration that [t]his opinion and its holding are confined" to those couples "joined in same-sex marriages made lawful by the State." [In] my opinion, however, the view that *this* Court will take of state prohibition of same-sex marriage is indicated beyond mistaking by today's opinion. As I have said, the real rationale of today's opinion [that] DOMA is motivated by "bare . . . desire to harm" couples in same-sex marriages.

[It] is hard to admit that one's political opponents are not monsters, especially in a struggle like this one, and the challenge in the end proves more than today's Court can handle. Too bad. A reminder that disagreement over something so fundamental as marriage can still be politically legitimate would have been a fit task for what in earlier times was called the judicial temperament. We might have covered ourselves with honor today, by promising all sides of this debate that it was theirs to settle and that we would respect their resolution. * * *

JUSTICE ALITO, with whom JUSTICE THOMAS joins in relevant part, dissenting.

[By] asking the Court to strike down DOMA as not satisfying some form of heightened scrutiny, Windsor and the United States are really seeking to have the Court resolve a debate between two competing views of marriage. The first and older view, which I will call the "traditional" or "conjugal" view, sees marriage as an intrinsically opposite-sex institution. [The] other, newer view is what I will call the "consent based" vision of marriage, a vision that primarily defines marriage as the solemnization of mutual commitment—marked by strong emotional attachment and sexual attraction—between two persons. [Proponents] of same-sex marriage argue that because gender differentiation is not relevant to this vision, the exclusion of same-sex couples from the institution of marriage is rank discrimination. The Constitution does not codify either of these views of marriage (although I suspect it would have been hard at the time of the adoption of the Constitution or the Fifth Amendment to find Americans who did not take the traditional view for granted). The silence of the Constitution on this question should be enough to end the matter as far as the judiciary is concerned. Yet, Windsor and the United States implicitly ask us to endorse the consent-based view of marriage and to reject the traditional view, thereby arrogating to ourselves the power to decide a question that philosophers, historians, social scientists, and theologians are better qualified to explore. Because our constitutional order assigns the resolution of questions of this nature to the people, I would not presume to enshrine either vision of marriage in our constitutional jurisprudence. * * *

On the same day that the Court decided *Windsor,* it dismissed the appeal in HOLLINGSWORTH v. PERRY, p. 75 of this Supplement, which sought reversal of a lower federal court decision that had restored state law same-sex marriage rights in Califormia after a citizen-initiated ballot proposition had withdrawn them, on standing grounds. The standing ruling had the effect of permitting same-sex couples to wed in California while avoiding any Court ruling on whether state prohibitions against same-sex marriage violate the Constitution.

II. ALIENAGE

P. 1475, at end of note 2

ARIZONA v. UNITED STATES, 132 S.Ct. 2492 (2012), per KENNEDY, J., relied on the Supremacy Clause and statutory preemption analysis to invalidate several provisions of a state statute targeted at aliens, including illegal aliens. Frustrated with what it viewed as lax federal enforcement of the immigration laws, Arizona enacted S.B. 1070 to "deter the unlawful entry and presence" of undocumented aliens. The Court emphasized that immigration was an area of special federal concern and that congressional regulation was "pervasive." Testing state law against federal law, it held that federal law preempted provisions of S.B. 1070 (1) imposing stiffer penalties than federal law for failing to carry federal registration documents, (2) making it a crime for unauthorized aliens to work when Congress had imposed criminal prohibitions on employers but not employees, and (3) giving broader authority to Arizona law enforcement personnel than federal law gives to federal officials to make warrantless arrests of suspected deportable aliens. These provisions created "obstacles" to Congress's objectives or otherwise contravened its aims in enacting less harsh legislation. But Kennedy, J., refused to strike down an Arizona requirement that, in order to verify immigration status with the federal government, state officers make reasonable attempts to determine the immigration status, before release, of persons that they lawfully stop and reasonably suspect of being in the United States illegally. The state law was unclear in several respects, he concluded, and a federal court should not strike it down until state courts had clarified what it meant. The Court did not, however, foreclose "other preemption and constitutional challenges to the law as interpreted and applied after it goes into effect," including challenges involving alleged unreasonable seizures in violation of the Fourth Amendment. "Arizona may have understandable frustrations with the problems caused by illegal immigration[,] but the State may not pursue policies that undermine federal law."

Scalia, Thomas, and Alito, JJ., each filed separate opinions dissenting from some or all of the Court's rulings of statutory invalidity. SCALIA, J., would have upheld S.B. 1070 in its entirety, because the authority to regulate immigration was not inherently federal: "Notwithstanding '[t]he myth of an era of unrestricted immigration' in the first 100 years of the Republic, the States enacted numerous laws restricting [immigration]." Because "the power to exclude" touched "the core of state sovereignty," Scalia, J., would not have found that Congress preempted state regulation unless it "unequivocally expres[sed]" its intent to do so. "The laws under challenge here do not extend or revise federal immigration restrictions, but merely enforce those restrictions more effectively. If securing its territory in this fashion is not within the power of Arizona, we should cease referring to it as a sovereign State."

Kagan, J., did not participate.

In another showdown involving the scope of state and federal prerogatives in immigration matters, ARIZONA v. INTER TRIBAL COUNCIL OF ARIZONA, 133 S.Ct. 2247 (2013), per SCALIA, J., held as a matter of statutory construction that a federal law that authorizes voter registration by mail and requires states to "accept and use" a federal registration form impliedly forbade Arizona to require would-be registrants to present documentary proof of citizenship. With respect to the constitutional issues that lingered in the background, involving the respective authority of the state and federal governments with respect to voting qualifications for participation in federal elections, the opinion emphasized that establishing substantive requirements for voting (such as citizenship) was a state matter under Art. I, sec. 2, cl. 1:

"[T]he Elections Clause, [Art. I, sec. 4, cl. 1,] empowers Congress to regulate *how* federal elections are held, but not *who* may vote in them." Accordingly, a serious constitutional question would be presented "if a federal statute precluded a State from obtaining information necessary to enforce its voter qualifications." Without determining whether a demand for documentary proof of citizenship was necessary to enforce Arizona's law, or whether the attestation required by the federal form would suffice, the Court noted that the federal statute at issue authorized Arizona to ask a federal agency to modify the voter registration form. It further noted the federal government's concession that the agency would be statutorily required to grant any modification "necessary" to enforce the state's substantive requirements. "Should [the federal agency fail to change the form], Arizona would have the opportunity to establish in a reviewing court that a mere oath will not suffice to effectuate its citizenship requirement.

ALITO, J., dissented on statutory grounds, arguing that Arizona's demand for supplementary documentation was consistent with the federal statutory requirement that it "accept and use" a federal form in registering voters. THOMAS, J., dissented on constitutional grounds: The State's constitutional authority "to determine the qualifications of voters in federal elections [necessarily] includes the related power to determine whether those qualifications are satisfied."

SECTION 5. FUNDAMENTAL RIGHTS

I. VOTING

B. "DILUTION" OF THE RIGHT: APPORTIONMENT

P. 1506, at the beginning of footnote a

Emphasizing a reviewing court's obligation to afford deference to a state legislature's "reasonable exercise of its political judgment," *Tennant v. Jefferson County Comm'n,* 133 S.Ct. 3 (2012), (per curiam) unanimously upheld a variance of 0.79% between West Virginia's largest and smallest districts in light of the state's legitimate interests in "avoiding contests between incumbents, [not] splitting political subdivisions," and minimizing populations shifts from one district to another.

D. "DILUTION" OF THE RIGHT: ISSUES INVOLVING RACE

P. 1526, at the end of the carryover paragraph

Shelby County v. Holder, discussed p. 68 of this Supplement, effectively rendered Section 5 of the Voting Rights Act inoperative by invalidating the "coverage" provision that made it applicable to some jurisdictions, which were initially specified in 1965, but not to others.

CHAPTER 11

CONGRESSIONAL ENFORCEMENT OF CIVIL RIGHTS

∎ ∎ ∎

SECTION 3. REGULATION OF STATE ACTORS

P. 1674, substitute for note (c)

(c) ***Changed circumstances over time.*** As discussed in *South Carolina v. Katzbach*, supra, the Voting Rights Act of 1965 "covered" those "States or political subdivisions that had maintained a test or device as a prerequisite to voting as of November 1, 1964, and had less than 50 percent voter registration or turnout in the 1964 Presidential election. Such tests or devices included literacy and knowledge tests, good moral character requirements, the need for vouchers from registered voters, and the like. §4(c). A covered jurisdiction could 'bail out' of coverage if it had not used a test or device in the preceding five years [later extended to ten years] 'for the purpose or with the effect of denying or abridging the right to vote on account of race or color.' §4(a). In 1965, the covered States included Alabama, Georgia, Louisiana, Mississippi, South Carolina, and Virginia. The additional covered subdivisions included 39 counties in North Carolina and one in Arizona.

"In those jurisdictions, §4 of the Act banned all such tests or devices. §4(a). Section 5 provided that no change in voting procedures could take effect until it was approved by federal authorities in Washington, D. C.— either the Attorney General or a court of three judges. A jurisdiction could obtain such 'preclearance' only by proving that the change had neither 'the purpose [nor] the effect of denying or abridging the right to vote on account of race or color.' "Sections 4 and 5 were intended to be temporary; they were set to expire after five years. [In] 1970, Congress reauthorized the Act for another five years, and extended the coverage formula in §4(b) to jurisdictions that had a voting test and less than 50 percent voter registration or turnout as of 1968. That swept in several counties in California, New Hampshire, and New York. Congress also extended the ban in §4(a) on tests and devices nationwide.

"In 1975, Congress reauthorized the Act for seven more years, and extended its coverage to jurisdictions that had a voting test and less than 50 percent voter registration or turnout as of 1972. Congress also amended the definition of 'test or device' to include the practice of providing English-only voting materials in places where over five percent of voting-age citizens spoke a single language other than English. As a result of these amendments, the

States of Alaska, Arizona, and Texas, as well as several counties in California, Florida, Michigan, New York, North Carolina, and South Dakota, became covered jurisdictions. Congress correspondingly amended sections 2 and 5 to forbid voting discrimination on the basis of membership in a language minority group. [Finally,] Congress made the nationwide ban on tests and devices permanent.

"In 1982, Congress reauthorized the Act for 25 years, but did not alter its coverage formula." This was repeated in 2006. Section 2, not at issue in this case, is applicable in all states and enforceable by both the federal government and by private individuals. It forbids any "standard, practice, or procedure" that "results in a denial or abridgement of the right of any citizen of the United States to vote on account of race or color." *Northwest Austin Municipal Utility Dist. v. Holder*, 557 U.S. 193 (2009), "expressed serious doubts about the Act's continued constitutionality," but construed the Act to avoid that issue. SHELBY COUNTY v. HOLDER, per ROBERTS, C.J., 133 S.Ct. 2612 (2013), held § 4 (the coverage formula required for preclearance under § 5) unconstitutional:

"In *Northwest Austin*, we stated that 'the Act imposes current burdens and must be justified by current needs.' And we concluded that 'a departure from the fundamental principle of equal sovereignty requires a showing that a statute's disparate geographic coverage is sufficiently related to the problem that it targets.' These basic principles guide our review of the question before us. [D]espite the tradition of equal sovereignty, the Act applies to only nine States (and several additional counties). [Even] if a noncovered jurisdiction is sued [under § 2], there are important differences between those proceedings and preclearance proceedings; the preclearance proceeding 'not only switches the burden of proof to the supplicant jurisdiction, but also applies substantive standards quite different from those governing the rest of the nation.' (Williams, J., dissenting) (case below). [As] we reiterated in *Northwest Austin*, the Act constitutes 'extraordinary legislation otherwise unfamiliar to our federal system.'

"[In 1966], the coverage formula—the means of linking the exercise of the unprecedented authority with the problem that warranted it—made sense. We found that 'Congress chose to limit its attention to the geographic areas where immediate action seemed necessary, where voting discrimination ha[d] been most flagrant.' Nearly 50 years later, things have changed dramatically. [In] the covered jurisdictions, '[v]oter turnout and registration rates now approach parity. Blatantly discriminatory evasions of federal decrees are rare. And minority candidates hold office at unprecedented levels.' *Northwest Austin.* * * * [The] House Report [noted] that '[i]n some circumstances, minorities register to vote and cast ballots at levels that surpass those of white voters.' [There] has been approximately a 1,000 percent increase since 1965 in the number of African-American elected officials in the six States originally covered by the Voting Rights Act.

"* * * Census Bureau data from the most recent election indicate that African-American voter turnout exceeded white voter turnout in five of the six States originally covered by §5, with a gap in the sixth State of less than one half of one percent. [In] the first decade after enactment of §5, the Attorney General objected to 14.2 percent of proposed voting changes. In the last decade before reenactment, the Attorney General objected to a mere 0.16 percent. There is no doubt that these improvements are in large part because of the Voting Rights Act. [Yet] the Act has not eased the restrictions in §5 or narrowed the scope of the coverage formula in §4(b) along the [way]—as if nothing had changed. In fact, the Act's unusual remedies have grown even stronger [as indicated supra. Under] this theory, however, §5 would be effectively immune from scrutiny; no matter how 'clean' the record of covered jurisdictions, the argument could always be made that it was deterrence that accounted for the good behavior. * * *

"Coverage today is based on decades-old data and eradicated practices. [In] 1965, the States could be divided into two groups: those with a recent history of voting tests and low voter registration and turnout, and those without those characteristics. Congress based its coverage formula on that distinction. Today the Nation is no longer divided along those lines, yet the Voting Rights Act continues to treat it as if it were. * * *

"The Fifteenth Amendment [is] not designed to punish for the past; its purpose is to ensure a better future. See *Rice v. Cayetano*, 528 U. S. 495, 512 (2000). To serve that purpose, Congress—if it is to divide the States—must identify those jurisdictions to be singled out on a basis that makes sense in light of current conditions. It cannot rely simply on the past. We made that clear in *Northwest Austin*, and we make it clear again [today.] Regardless of how to look at the record, [no] one can fairly say that it shows anything approaching the 'pervasive,' 'flagrant,' 'widespread,' and 'rampant' discrimination that faced Congress in 1965, and that clearly distinguished the covered jurisdictions from the rest of the Nation at that time. But a more fundamental problem remains: Congress did not use the record it compiled to shape a coverage formula grounded in current conditions. It instead reenacted a formula based on 40-year-old facts having no logical relation to the present day.

"[If] Congress had started from scratch in 2006, it plainly could not have enacted the present coverage formula. It would have been irrational for Congress to distinguish between States in such a fundamental way based on 40-year-old data, when today's statistics tell an entirely different story. And it would have been irrational to base coverage on the use of voting tests 40 years ago, when such tests have been illegal since that time. But that is exactly what Congress has done.

"* * * We issue no holding on §5 itself, only on the coverage formula. Congress may draft another formula based on current conditions. Such a formula is an initial prerequisite to a determination that exceptional conditions still exist justifying such an 'extraordinary departure from the traditional course of relations between the States and the Federal Government.' "[dd]

GINSBURG, J., joined by Breyer, Sotomayor, and Kagan JJ., dissented in a long and greatly detailed opinion, pointing to "volumes of evidence" Congress considered, including "large numbers of proposed changes to voting laws that the Attorney General declined to approve"; the emergence of " 'second generation barriers' to minority voting" (those that "reduce the impact of minority votes, in contrast to direct attempts to block access to the ballot," (such as "racial gerrymandering," "a system of at-large voting in lieu of district-by-district voting," and "discriminatory annexation [of] majority-white areas into city limits").

In response to the Court's statistics, "between 1982 and 2006, DOJ objections blocked over 700 voting changes based on a determination that the changes were discriminatory. Congress found that the majority of DOJ objections included findings of discriminatory intent, and that the changes blocked by preclearance were 'calculated decisions to keep minority voters from fully participating in the political process.' * * * Congress received evidence that more than 800 proposed changes were altered or withdrawn since the last reauthorization in 1982. Congress also received empirical studies finding that DOJ's requests for more information had a significant effect on the degree to which covered jurisdictions 'compl[ied] with their obligatio[n]' to protect minority voting rights. Congress also received evidence that litigation under §2 of the VRA was an inadequate substitute for preclearance in the covered jurisdictions. [This evidence] of preclearance's continuing efficacy in blocking constitutional violations in the covered jurisdictions, itself grounded Congress' conclusion that the remedy should be retained for those jurisdictions.

"[A study] of § 2 lawsuits in covered and noncovered jurisdictions indicated that racial discrimination in voting remains 'concentrated in the jurisdictions singled out for preclearance.'

[The] evidence before Congress, furthermore, indicated that voting in the covered jurisdictions was more racially polarized than elsewhere in the country. [Moreover,] Congress was satisfied that the VRA's bailout mechanism provided an effective means of adjusting the VRA's coverage over time. [T]he Court does not even deign to grapple with the legislative record. [In] 2008, for example, the city of Calera, located in Shelby County, requested preclearance of a redistricting plan that 'would have eliminated the city's sole majority-black district, which had been created pursuant to the consent decree.' [Although] DOJ objected to the plan, Calera forged ahead with elections based on the unprecleared voting changes, resulting in the defeat of the incumbent African-American councilman who represented the former majority-black district. The city's defiance required DOJ to bring a §5 enforcement action that ultimately yielded appropriate redress, including

---

[dd] Thomas, J., concurred on the ground that the Court's opinion "compellingly demonstrates" that § 5 is also unconstitutional.

restoration of the majority-black district. [These] recent episodes forcefully demonstrate that §5's preclearance requirement is constitutional as applied to Alabama and its political subdivisions. And under our case law, that conclusion should suffice to resolve this case.

"[Under the] VRA's exceptionally broad severability provision, [even] if the VRA could not constitutionally be applied to certain States—e.g., Arizona and Alaska, it calls for those unconstitutional applications to be severed, leaving the Act in place for jurisdictions as to which its application does not transgress constitutional limits. * * * Leaping to resolve Shelby County's facial challenge without considering whether application of the VRA to Shelby County is constitutional, or even addressing the VRA's severability provision, the Court's opinion can hardly be described as an exemplar of restrained and moderate decisionmaking.

"[Today's] unprecedented extension of the equal sovereignty principle outside its proper domain—the admission of new States—is capable of much mischief. Federal statutes that treat States disparately are hardly novelties [citing 7 federal statutes as examples].

"[The] situation Congress faced in 2006, when it took up reauthorization of the coverage formula, was not the same [as in 1965]. By then, the formula had been in effect for many years, and *all* of the jurisdictions covered by it were 'familiar to Congress by name.' [There] was at that point no chance that the formula might inadvertently sweep in new areas that were not the subject of congressional findings. And Congress could determine from the record whether the jurisdictions captured by the coverage formula still belonged under the preclearance regime. If they did, there was no need to alter the formula. That is why the Court, in addressing prior reauthorizations of the VRA, did not question the continuing 'relevance' of the formula. [In] light of this record, Congress had more than a reasonable basis to conclude that the existing coverage formula was not out of sync with conditions on the ground in covered areas.

"[The] question this case presents is who decides whether, as currently operative, §5 remains justifiable, this Court, or a Congress charged with the obligation to enforce the post-Civil War Amendments. [The] record supporting the 2006 reauthorization of the VRA [was] described by the Chairman of the House Judiciary Committee as 'one of the most extensive considerations of any piece of legislation that the United States Congress has dealt with in the 27½ years' he had served in the House. [With] overwhelming support in both Houses, Congress concluded that, for two prime reasons, §5 should continue in force, unabated. First, continuance would facilitate completion of the impressive gains thus far made; and second, continuance would guard against backsliding. [That] determination of the body empowered to enforce the Civil War Amendments 'by appropriate legislation' merits this Court's utmost respect. In my judgment, the Court errs egregiously by overriding Congress' decision."

P. 1689, add before note (b) at bottom of page:

Compare: COLEMAN v. MARYLAND COURT OF APPEALS, 132 S.Ct. 1327 (2012) per KENNEDY, J., joined by Roberts, C.J., and Thomas and Alito, JJ., held that the FMLA provision for unpaid leave for "self-care" was beyond Congress's § 5 power because, unlike the "well-documented pattern of sex-based discrimination in family-leave policies [in] *Hibbs*, the self-care provision was not directed at an identified pattern of gender-based discrimination and was not congruent and proportional."[d]

GINSBURG, J., joined by Breyer, Sotomayor and Kagan, JJ., dissented.[e] "The FMLA, in its entirety, is directed at sex discrimination [and] Congress has evidence of a well-documented pattern of workplace discrimination against pregnant women. [Because] pregnancy discrimination is inevitably sex discrimination, and because discrimination against women is tightly interwoven with society's beliefs about pregnancy and motherhood, I [believe] that [*Geduldig v. Aiello*, Ch. 9, Sec. 3, II] was egregiously wrong to hold that discrimination on the basis of pregnancy is not discrimination on the basis of sex. [It] would make scant sense to provide job-protected leave for a woman to care for a newborn, but not [for] 'ongoing pregnancy, miscarriages, . . . the need for prenatal care, childbirth, and recovery from childbirth.' * * *

"If Congress had drawn a line at leave for caring for other family members, there is greater likelihood that the FMLA would have been perceived [by employers] as further reason to avoid granting employment opportunities to women.' [In] other words, 'the availability of self-care leave to men serves to blunt the force of stereotypes of women as primary caregivers by increasing the odds that men and women will invoke the FMLA's leave provisions in near-equal numbers.' [By] reducing an employer's perceived incentive to avoid hiring women [the self care provision] lessens the risk that the FMLA as a whole would give rise to the very sex discrimination it was enacted to thwart."

---

[d] Scalia, J., concurred only in the judgment based on his opinion in *Tennessee v. Lane*, infra.

[e] Ginsburg, J., joined only by Breyer, J., expressed her continued disagreement with *Seminole Tribe* and *Garrett*.

CHAPTER 12

LIMITATIONS ON JUDICIAL POWER AND REVIEW

■ ■ ■

SECTION 2. STANDING

I. THE STRUCTURE OF STANDING DOCTRINE

P. 1716, at the end of note 4

(d) *Threatened future injuries.* When a party cannot credibly demonstrate past injury, but seeks injunctive relief to prevent a threatened future injury, how certain or imminent does the threat of future injury need to be to ground standing? In CLAPPER v. AMNESTY INTERNATIONAL, 133 S.Ct. 1138 (2013), U.S. citizens residing in the United States challenged the constitutionality of an amendment to the Foreign Intelligence Surveillance Act under which, they alleged, their communications with non-Americans abroad were likely to be intercepted. The Court, per ALITO, J., denied standing based on the plaintiffs' failure to establish that an injury-in-fact was "certainly impending" in light, inter alia, of the opacity of the Government's criteria for seeking foreign-security wiretaps: "[W]e have often found a lack of standing in cases in which the Judiciary has been requested to review actions of the political branches in the fields of intelligence gathering and foreign affairs. [The] assumption that if respondents have no standing to sue, no one would have standing, is not a reason to find standing." BREYER, J., joined by Ginsburg, Sotomayor, and Kagan, JJ., dissenting, maintained that although some past Court decisions had referred to a need for "certainly impending" injury, future injury was seldom if ever "absolutely certain" and that "federal courts frequently [and appropriately] entertain actions for injunctions and for declaratory relief aimed at preventing future injures that are reasonably likely or highly likely [to] take place."

P. 1719, at end of footnote h

Bond v. United States, 131 S.Ct. 2355 (2011), per Kennedy, J., held that a criminal defendant challenging the constitutionality of a federal statute on the ground that it exceeded congressional authority under Article I and the Tenth Amendment asserted personal rights, not those of the states, and that the third-party standing doctrine therefore posed no impediment to suit: "States are not the sole intended beneficiaries of federalism." Ginsburg, J., joined by Breyer, J., concurred: "Bond, like any other defendant, has a personal right not to be convicted under a constitutionally invalid law."

III. TAXPAYER STANDING AND OTHER STATUS–BASED STANDING ISSUES

P. 1731, add after top paragraph

The Court continued reading *Flast* ever more narrowly in ARIZONA CHRISTIAN SCHOOL TUITION ORG. v. WINN, 131 S.Ct. 1436 (2011), per KENNEDY, J., holding that taxpayers lack standing to challenge dollar-for-dollar tax credits for contributions to organizations that provide scholarships to children attending religious schools: "A dissenter whose tax dollars are 'extracted and spent' knows that he has in some small measure been made to contribute to an establishment of religion in violation of conscience. *Flast*. [By contrast, a] tax credit is not tantamount to a religious tax and does not visit the injury identified in *Flast*." KAGAN, J., joined by Ginsburg, Breyer, and Sotomayor, JJ., dissented: In five previous cases challenging tax credits that subsidize religion, "we have [always] resolved the suit without questioning the plaintiffs' standing. [The] Court's opinion [offers] a roadmap—more truly, just a one-step instruction—to any government that wishes to insulate its financing of religious activity from legal challenge. Structure the funding as a tax expenditure, and *Flast* will not stand in the way."

P. 1733, after note 6

7. ***Standing to defend laws against constitutional challenge.*** When a party sues to enjoin a federal or state law on the ground that it violates the Constitution, one or more government officials will always have standing to defend the law. Complex issues can arise if responsible officials elect not to defend a challenged law, but some other party wishes to do so.

In UNITED STATES v. WINDSOR, p. 58 of this Supplement, the President and Attorney General concluded that the provision of the federal Defense of Marriage Act (DOMA) that denies federal recognition to gay marriages was unconstitutional and notified Congress that they would not defend it in court against constitutional attack. But the Administration, though not defending DOMA in court, continued to enforce it, in order to let the courts determine DOMA's constitutionality. Consequently, the House of Representatives authorized its Bipartisan Legal Advisory Group (BLAG) to intervene on its behalf, as BLAG did in a case brought by Windsor. When the district court and the court of appeals both held DOMA unconstitutional in pertinent part, the United States and BLAG both sought certiorari. On its own motion, the Court appointed an amica curiae to argue the position that the Court lacked jurisdiction to hear the dispute because the United States agreed with Windsor about the constitutional issue.

The Court, per KENNEDY, J., upheld the standing of the United States to seek review. All agreed that the district court had jurisdiction over Windsor's suit to recover money she had lost as a result of the government's refusing to treat her as the "spouse" of her deceased partner. And the Court reasoned that "the United States retains a stake sufficient to support Article III jurisdiction on appeal [because the judgment below] orders the United States to pay Windsor the refund she seeks" and the United States refused to pay it: "[It] would be a different case if the Executive had taken the further step of paying Windsor the refund." Having concluded that the United States satisfied the Article III requisites for jurisdiction, the Court noted that its exercise of jurisdiction was also governed by "prudential" considerations, but determined that the presence of BLAG as an intervenor, and its "sharp adversarial presentation of the issues satisfies the prudential concerns that otherwise might counsel against hearing an appeal from a decision with which the principal parties agree. Were this Court to hold that prudential rules require it to dismiss the case, and, in consequence, that the Court of Appeals erred in failing to dismiss it as well, extensive litigation would ensue. The district courts in 94 districts throughout the Nation would be without precedential guidance not only in tax refund suits but also in cases involving the whole of DOMA's sweep involving over 1,000 federal statutes and a myriad of federal regulations." The Court found it unnecessary to decide whether BLAG might have had standing to appeal in its own right.

SCALIA, J., joined by Roberts, C.J., and Thomas, J., dissented: "Article III requires not just a plaintiff (or appellant) who has standing to complain but *an opposing party* who denies the validity of the complaint. [The] question here is not whether, as the majority puts it, 'the United States retains a stake sufficient to support Article III jurisdiction,' the question is whether there is any controversy (which requires *contradiction*) between the United States and Ms. Windsor. There is not.

"[It] may be argued that if what we say is true some Presidential determinations that statutes are unconstitutional will not be subject to our review. That is as it should be, when both the President and the plaintiff agree that the statute is unconstitutional."

ALITO, J., agreed with Scalia, J., that the United States lacked standing to appeal, but he thought that BLAG did: "[In] the narrow category of cases in which a court strikes down an Act of Congress and the Executive declines to defend the Act, Congress both has standing to defend the undefended statute and is a proper party to do so." Roberts, C.J., joined by Scalia, and Thomas, JJ., dissented.

———————

HOLLINGSWORTH v. PERRY, 133 S.Ct. 2652 (2013), presented a partly parallel issue. Elected California officials declined to defend a ballot proposition enacted by California voters, entitled Proposition 8, that amended the California constitution to define marriage as a union between a man and a woman. The district court allowed the official proponents of the initiative to intervene to defend it, but ruled Proposition 8 unconstitutional on the merits. After receiving a certification from the California Supreme Court that "[i]n a postelection challenge to a voter-approved initiative measure, the official proponents are authorized under California law to appear and assert the state's interest in the initiative's validity," the court of appeals allowed the proponents to appeal but also concluded that Proposition 8 violated the Constitution.

The Court, per ROBERTS, C.J., dismissed for lack of standing: "No one doubts that a State has a cognizable interest 'in the continued enforceability' of its laws that is harmed by a judicial decision declaring a state law unconstitutional. To vindicate that interest or any other, a State must be able to designate agents to represent it in federal court." But petitioners were neither state officials nor agents: "[T]he most basic features of an agency relationship are missing here. [No] provision provides for [removal]." Accordingly, "petitioners had no 'direct stake' in the outcome of their appeal. Their only interest in having the District Court order reversed was to vindicate the constitutional validity of a generally applicable California law. [The] fact that a State [through its Supreme Court], thinks a private party should have standing to seek relief for a generalized grievance cannot override our settled law to the contrary."

KENNEDY, J., dissenting, joined by Thomas, Alito and Sotomayor, JJ., argued that California state law "defin[ing] and elaborat[ing] the status of an initiative's proponents who seek to intervene in court to defend the initiative after its adoption" was consistent with federal constitutional requirements and thus controlling: "The initiative's 'primary purpose [was] to afford the people the ability to propose and to adopt constitutional amendments or statutory provisions that their elected public officials had refused or declined to adopt.' The California Supreme Court has determined that this purpose is undermined if the very officials the initiative process seeks to circumvent are the only parties who can defend an enacted initiative when it is challenged in a legal proceeding." Nothing in Article III required rejection of this determination: "[T]he Court today concludes that this state-defined status and this state-conferred right fall short of meeting federal requirements because the proponents cannot point to a formal delegation of authority that tracks the requirements of the Restatement of Agency. But the State Supreme Court's definition of proponents' powers is binding on this Court. And that definition is fully sufficient to establish the standing and adversity that are requisites for justiciability under Article III."

SECTION 3. TIMING OF ADJUDICATION

I. MOOTNESS

P. 1737, at end of note 2

The Court applied the capable of repetition, yet evading review doctrine in *Turner v. Rogers*, 131 S.Ct. 2507 (2011), involving whether the Due Process Clause creates a right to appointed counsel for indigents facing incarceration in civil contempt proceedings. The Court found "more than a 'reasonable' likelihood" that Turner, who had been the subject of several such proceedings based on non-payment of child support, would again be subject to them in the future. Because the 12–month maximum sentence was too brief for Turner to bring his constitutional claims before the Court during any particular period of incarceration, the dispute was capable of repetition, yet evading review.

P. 1738, add footnote at end of note 4

e. But cf. *Genesis Healthcare Corp. v. Symczyk*, 133 S.Ct. 1523 (2013) (holding, 5–4, that mootness doctrine required dismissal of a "collective action" under the Fair Labor Standards Act when a named plaintiff's personal claim had already become moot before she moved for "provisional certification" of a class).